# Academic Library Value

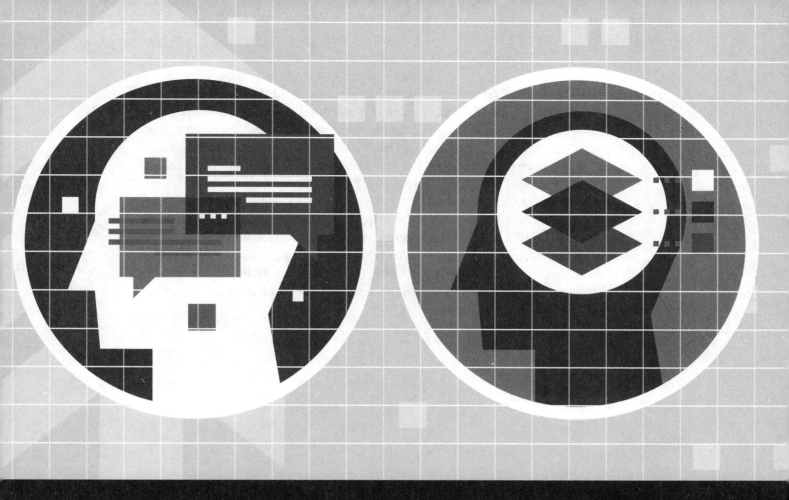

# Academic Library Value
## THE IMPACT STARTER KIT

*Megan Oakleaf*

ala
editions

An imprint of the American Library Association
CHICAGO 2017

**MEGAN OAKLEAF** is an Associate Professor in the Syracuse University iSchool. The author of ACRL's *Value of Academic Libraries: A Comprehensive Review and Report*, she has published in top library and information science journals including College and Research Libraries, Portal, JASIST, and *Journal of Documentation*. Megan has presented at numerous conferences, including ALA, ACRL, AAC&U, and AALHE national conferences, the Library Assessment Conference, the IUPUI Assessment Institute, and EDUCAUSE. Megan won the 2011 Ilene Rockman Publication of the Year award, was included in the LIRT Top 20 Instruction Articles five times, earned Best Paper recognition at the 2007 EBLIP conference, and was awarded the 2014 Jeffrey Katzer Teacher of the Year award. Her research areas include library value, learning analytics, rubric assessment, and information literacy instruction.

© 2012, 2017 by Megan Oakleaf

Extensive effort has gone into ensuring the reliability of the information in this book; however, the publisher makes no warranty, express or implied, with respect to the material contained herein.

ISBN: 978-0-8389-1592-9 (paper)

**Library of Congress Cataloging-in-Publication Data**
Names: Oakleaf, Megan J., author.
Title: Academic library value : the impact starter kit / Megan Oakleaf.
Description: Chicago : ALA Editions, an imprint of the American Library Association, 2017.
Identifiers: LCCN 2017022138 | ISBN 9780838915929 (pbk. : alk. paper)
Subjects: LCSH: Academic libraries—Evaluation—Problems, exercises, etc. | Academic
    libraries—Relations with faculty and curriculum—Problems, exercises, etc. | Libraries and
    colleges—Problems, exercises, etc.
Classification: LCC Z675.U5 O15 2017 | DDC 027.7--dc23 LC record available at https://lccn
    .loc.gov/2017022138

Cover design by Kimberly Thornton. Text composition by Alejandra Diaz in the Cardea and Proxima Nova typefaces.

♾ This paper meets the requirements of ANSI/NISO Z39.48-1992 (Permanence of Paper).

Printed in the United States of America
21  20  19  18  17      5  4  3  2  1

# CONTENTS

## FOCUSING ON IMPACT

## GETTING TO WORK

## COMMUNICATING & DECISION-MAKING

# PREFACE

In 2010, I authored *The Value of Academic Libraries: A Comprehensive Research Review and Report*, published by the Association of College and Research Libraries (ACRL). This report defined academic library value in the context of overarching higher education institutions, summarized existing literature on library value, recommended "next steps" for libraries seeking to extend and improve their value, and outlined a research agenda for future investigations of library value. Because ACRL intended the report to address a national academic library audience, I did not provide a single solution for individual libraries seeking to increase their value. Rather, I described a variety of options that libraries may evaluate, select, and adapt to their local contexts and unique needs. Consequently, the task of tailoring general library value concepts to specific libraries initially fell to individual librarians.

As the author of *The Value of Academic Libraries* report, I have worked extensively with librarians to help them apply value and impact concepts to their individual libraries. As I designed professional development and worked in consultancy roles, I developed a number of concepts, exercises, and practices that helped librarians customize the broader lessons of the report. Over time, I collected and refined these activities and sequenced them according to the needs of individual libraries. In 2012, hoping to share the activities with a broader audience, I self-published *Academic Library Value: The Impact Starter Kit* as a companion workbook for *The Value of Academic Libraries* report. This reprint edition continues the publication with a new design and format.

At the time of this printing, the pursuit of academic library value creation, demonstration, and communication continues. ACRL has commissioned an update to the 2010 report, entitled *The Action-Oriented Research Agenda on Library Contributions to Student Learning and Success*. Currently, the penultimate draft of the 2017 update is available. It includes a literature review of academic library value literature published since 2010, a summary of focus groups and interviews conducted with a small number of higher education administrators, and a list of priority areas of future research. Recommended areas for future research include: communication, collaboration, institutional planning, learning, success, and learning analytics. These areas represent a continuation and narrowing of the focus of the 2010 report, but do not suggest a change in the direction of the academic library value research trajectory. Finally, the update will include visualizations designed to help librarians access publications published on academic library value from 2010–2016, but that component is not yet available for review.

Both *The Value of Academic Libraries* report and the 2017 update offer librarians a guide to the pursuit of academic library value. As relevant, practical, and needed as ever, this workbook augments that work by providing a series of 52 activities intended to assist librarians as they conceptualize library value, identify existing library value, and increase library value in the context of their institutional missions.

Each activity helps librarians:

- rethink, refine, or redefine the value of their library within their institutional environment;
- identify and listen to institutional stakeholders;
- organize and manage new approaches to addressing library value; or
- take action to assess, expand, and communicate library value in order to position their library as an increasingly valuable asset to their overarching institution.

Four ideas, depicted in the library impact model, underpin the activities presented in *Academic Library Value: The Impact Starter Kit.*

1. The activities focus primarily on impact as a key facet of academic library value—namely, the difference academic libraries and librarians make in the lives of their stakeholders.
2. The activities emphasize *institutional focus areas,* or the specific needs, goals, and outcomes of individual community colleges, colleges, and universities where library impact is most needed.
3. The activities present libraries as multidimensional organizations that provide valuable *services, expertise,* and *resources,* all of which can impact institutional focus areas.
4. The activities position the *assessment* of library impact on institutional focus areas as central to the work of librarians—a professional value aligned with reflective, evidence-based, and pragmatic practice.

Each activity also includes a list of Suggested Readings. Some readings direct librarians to the relevant portions of the 2010 report, which can serve as a primer in academic library value concepts; others point to articles that inspired my thinking and shaped the activities. I encourage all librarians to visit the ACRL's Value of Academic Libraries website to learn about and engage with ongoing academic library value research and discussion: www.acrl.ala.org/value.

Used in conjunction with *The Value of Academic Libraries: A Comprehensive Research Review and Report* and *The Action-Oriented Research Agenda on Library Contributions to Student Learning and Success*, the activities found in *Academic Library Value: The Impact Starter Kit* offer support and guidance for academic librarians seeking to define the value of their libraries, align library value with stakeholder needs, deploy new strategies to increase and communicate library value, and ensure their library's position as a key contributor to achieving the mission of their institutions, now and in the future.

## Library Impact Model

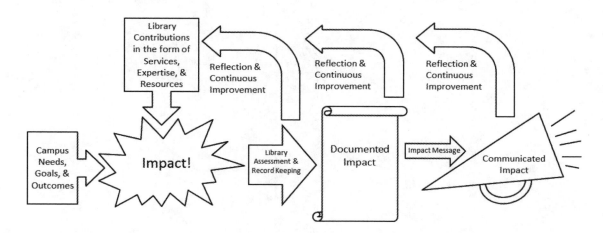

Adapted from: Oakleaf, Megan. "Are They Learning? Are We? Learning and the Academic Library." *Library Quarterly*. 81(1). 2011. 61–82.

# HOW TO USE THIS BOOK

*Academic Library Value: The Impact Starter Kit* includes 52 activities designed to help librarians as they define library value, assess existing library value, and expand library value in the context of institutional missions.

## Where Do I Start?

The activities can be engaged in a variety of ways:

- **Option #1:** Complete the activities in numerical order, beginning with Activity #1: Institutional Focus Areas.
- **Option #2:** Complete the activities by theme. There are four themes designated by graphics at the beginning of each activity: Re-thinking, Listening, Getting Organized, and Taking Action.
- **Option #3:** Complete the activities in order of interest, organizational goal, or professional development need.

## How Do I Approach Each Activity?

1. Consider the purpose ("Goal") and rationale ("Why") for the activity.
2. Read the instructions ("Directions") for the activity.
3. Optional: Skim any background material ("Suggested Readings").
4. Optional: Review any cross-referenced ("See Also") activities.
5. Unfold the page and complete the activity.
6. When the activity is complete, engage the **T3 process** on the back of each page.

## Should I Complete These Activities Independently or with a Group?

Most activities can be completed either alone or with others; only a few require partners. However, the ideas generated by these activities multiply when shared with colleagues! Consequently, librarians may wish to share the activities with entire units, committees, or departments.

**Should I use these activities in professional development contexts?**

These activities can be used as professional development tools for self-paced instruction or training sessions led locally or by outside consultants. The author is available to lead training sessions using these activities. For more information, go to www.meganoakleaf.info.

# INSTITUTIONAL FOCUS AREAS

## Goal
Identify focus areas relevant to an institution.

## Why
To redefine library value in the context of institutional needs, goals, and outcomes, librarians need to identify what is most important to their institution.

## Directions
1. Consider institutional focus areas; add any that are missing.
2. Check off institutional focus areas that are relevant to your institution.
3. Consider the checked institutional focus areas. Circle the five areas that are most important to your institution.
4. List them in rank order. This is your core institutional focus area list.
5. Engage the **T3** process.

## Suggested Readings
Oakleaf, Megan. *The Value of Academic Libraries: A Comprehensive Research Review and Report.* Chicago: ACRL, 2010. 26–30, 94.

Oakleaf, Megan. "Are They Learning? Are We? Learning and the Academic Library." *Library Quarterly.* 81(1). 2011. 61–82.

> 66 Few libraries exist in a vacuum, accountable only to themselves. There is always a larger context for assessing library quality, that is, what and how well does the library contribute to achieving the overall goals of the parent constituencies?"
>
> —SARAH PRITCHARD

## Institutional Focus Areas

### Student
○ Student Recruitment, Enrollment
○ Student Retention, Completion, Graduation
○ Student Career Success
○ Student GPA, Test Achievement
○ Student Learning Outcomes
○ Student Experience, Engagement
○ Student-Faculty Academic Rapport
○ Alumni Lifelong Learning

○ Other: _____
○ Other: _____

### Faculty
○ Faculty Recruitment, Tenure, Promotion
○ Faculty Teaching
○ Faculty Service
○ Faculty Research Productivity
○ Faculty Grant Seeking
○ Faculty Patents, Technology Transfer
○ Faculty Innovation, Entrepreneurship

○ Other: _____
○ Other: _____

### Institution
○ Institutional Prestige
○ Institutional Affordability
○ Institutional Efficiencies
○ Institutional Accreditation, Program Review
○ Institutional Brand
○ Institutional Athletics
○ Institutional Development, Funding, Endowments

○ Other: _____
○ Other: _____

## Community

○ Local, Global Workforce Development

○ Local, Global Economic Growth

○ Local, Global Engagement, Community-Building, Social Inclusion

○ Other: _____

○ Other: _____

## Top Institutional Focus Areas

1. _____

2. _____

3. _____

4. _____

5. _____

**THINK**      How did this activity make me feel?

_____

_____

What questions do I have?

_____

_____

What do I want to learn more about?

_____

_____

What innovative ideas have emerged?

_____

_____

**TALK**      What does this mean for my library? For me, as a librarian?

_____

_____

What do we need to do differently, as a library?

_____

_____

What does this make me want to continue to do, do better, or do differently, as a librarian?

_____

_____

**TARGET**

| Action | Timeframe | Responsible Parties | Follow-Up |
|---|---|---|---|
| **Options to Consider**<br>• Contact colleague<br>• Make decision<br>• Take action<br>• Ask question<br>• Get evidence/data | **When to Do It**<br>• Today<br>• This week<br>• This month<br>• This semester<br>• This year<br>• 2-3 year plan | **Who to Involve**<br>• Students<br>• Staff<br>• Librarians<br>• Administrators<br>• Faculty | **What to Do Next**<br>After I complete this action, what's the next step? |
|  |  |  |  |
|  |  |  |  |
|  |  |  |  |
|  |  |  |  |
|  |  |  |  |

ACTIVITY #2

# STAKEHOLDERS AS THE HEART OF THE INSTITUTION

## Goal

Focus attention on stakeholders.

## Why

To understand the impact of the library on stakeholders, librarians need to identify their stakeholder groups.

## Directions

1. Consider major stakeholder categories; add any that are missing.
2. Check off those groups that are relevant to your institution.
3. Consider the checked stakeholder groups. Circle the five groups that are most important to your institution. This is your core institutional stakeholder list.
4. Engage the **T3** process.

## Suggested Reading

Oakleaf, Megan. *The Value of Academic Libraries: A Comprehensive Research Review and Report.* Chicago: ACRL, 2010. 26–28.

## Students

○ High school
○ Prospective
○ First-year
○ Majors
○ International

○ Co-curricular groups
○ First generation
○ Honors
○ At-risk
○ Graduate

○ Nontraditional
○ Veterans
○ Distance/Online
○ Transfer

○ _____

○ _____

○ _____

## Faculty

○ Tenured/tenure
  track faculty
○ Non-tenure track faculty

○ Research faculty
○ Part-time faculty
○ Adjunct faculty

○ Instructors/lecturers
○ Teaching assistants

○ _____

○ _____

○ _____

## Parents

○ Of first-year students
○ Of first-generation students

○ _____

○ _____

○ _____

## Student Affairs

○ Admissions
○ Tutorial services

○ Residence life
○ Study abroad

○ Greek life
○ Athletics

○ _____

○ _____

○ _____

## Institutional Offices

- ○ Sponsored programs
- ○ Human subjects
- ○ Educational assessment
- ○ Institutional research

- ○ _____
- ○ _____
- ○ _____

## Administration

- ○ Presidents/chancellors/provosts
- ○ Deans
- ○ Faculty senate
- ○ Department/unit heads
- ○ Committee chairs

- ○ _____
- ○ _____
- ○ _____

## Accreditors

- ○ Regional
- ○ Professional

- ○ _____
- ○ _____
- ○ _____

## Employers

- ○ _____
- ○ _____
- ○ _____

## Graduate Schools

- ○ _____
- ○ _____
- ○ _____

## Local Community

○ K–12 schools  ○ Local government
○ Business owners  ○ General populace

○ _____

○ _____

○ _____

## State Community

○ State government

○ _____

○ _____

○ _____

## National Community

○ Federal government

○ _____

○ _____

○ _____

## Funders

○ Granting agencies
○ Alumni
○ Donors

○ _____

○ _____

○ _____

## Library

- ○ Library administration
- ○ Librarians
- ○ Library support staff
- ○ Student employees

- ○ Consortial partners
- ○ Professional associations
- ○ Larger professional community

- ○ _____
- ○ _____
- ○ _____

## Top Stakeholder Groups

1. _____
2. _____
3. _____
4. _____
5. _____

**THINK**

How did this activity make me feel?

_____

_____

What questions do I have?

_____

_____

What do I want to learn more about?

_____

_____

What innovative ideas have emerged?

_____

_____

**TALK**

What does this mean for my library? For me, as a librarian?

_____

_____

What do we need to do differently, as a library?

_____

_____

What does this make me want to continue to do, do better, or do differently, as a librarian?

_____

_____

**TARGET**

| Action | Timeframe | Responsible Parties | Follow-Up |
|---|---|---|---|
| **Options to Consider**<br>• Contact colleague<br>• Make decision<br>• Take action<br>• Ask question<br>• Get evidence/data | **When to Do It**<br>• Today<br>• This week<br>• This month<br>• This semester<br>• This year<br>• 2-3 year plan | **Who to Involve**<br>• Students<br>• Staff<br>• Librarians<br>• Administrators<br>• Faculty | **What to Do Next**<br>After I complete this action, what's the next step? |
| | | | |
| | | | |
| | | | |
| | | | |
| | | | |

# STAKEHOLDER ROLE PLAY

RE-THINKING

### Goal
Brainstorm "what matters" to targeted stakeholder groups.

### Why
To serve stakeholders, librarians need to understand their goals, needs, and desired outcomes.

### Directions
1. Find two partners; you need three people for this activity.
2. Pick a stakeholder group to focus on.
3. Assign roles: interviewer, stakeholder, and recorder.
4. Give each partner the section for his/her role.
5. Allow time for the "stakeholder" to embody his/her role.
6. Interview the "stakeholder" and record his/her responses.
7. As a group, analyze "what matters" to this stakeholder.
8. As a group, brainstorm ways the library can contribute to "what matters" to this stakeholder group.
9. Rotate roles and repeat for another stakeholder group.
10. Engage the **T3** process.

### Suggested Reading
Oakleaf, Megan. *The Value of Academic Libraries: A Comprehensive Research Review and Report.* Chicago: ACRL, 2010. 26–28.

### See Also
Activity #2: Stakeholders as the Heart of the Institution

### "Interviewer" Script

Stakeholder Group: _____

### Questions

1. Why are you attending, working at, or involved with this institution?
2. What are your goals? What are you trying to accomplish? What matters to you? What are your needs?
3. What do you want to result from your time at or in connection with this institution?
4. What do you need to be successful at or in connection with this institution?
5. What are the biggest challenges facing you?
6. What kind of information/resources/data/evidence do you need to be successful and overcome challenges?

Other: _____

_____

_____

_____

### "Stakeholder" Prep

Stakeholder Group: _____

*Congratulations!* You have been selected to pretend to be a member of the stakeholder group listed above.

**The Challenge:** To truly embody a member of this stakeholder group, imagine yourself as a member of the group. How old are you? What are your interests? Your work/school goals? What is your connection to this institution? What do you want to gain from the connection?

Now prepare to perform—and stay "in character"!

_____

_____

_____

_____

## "Recorder" Notes

Stakeholder Group: _____

What matters to this stakeholder?

_____

_____

_____

_____

_____

_____

_____

## Analysis

Stakeholder Group: _____

In short, what are the needs, goals, and desired outcomes of this "stakeholder"?

_____

_____

_____

What existing library services, expertise, or resources could benefit this stakeholder group?

_____

_____

_____

What library services, expertise, or resources could/should be developed to benefit this stakeholder group?

_____

_____

_____

**THINK**

How did this activity make me feel?

_____

_____

What questions do I have?

_____

_____

What do I want to learn more about?

_____

_____

What innovative ideas have emerged?

_____

_____

**TALK**

What does this mean for my library? For me, as a librarian?

_____

_____

What do we need to do differently, as a library?

_____

_____

What does this make me want to continue to do, do better, or do differently, as a librarian?

_____

_____

**TARGET**

| Action | Timeframe | Responsible Parties | Follow-Up |
|---|---|---|---|
| **Options to Consider**<br>• Contact colleague<br>• Make decision<br>• Take action<br>• Ask question<br>• Get evidence/data | **When to Do It**<br>• Today<br>• This week<br>• This month<br>• This semester<br>• This year<br>• 2-3 year plan | **Who to Involve**<br>• Students<br>• Staff<br>• Librarians<br>• Administrators<br>• Faculty | **What to Do Next**<br>After I complete this action, what's the next step? |
| | | | |
| | | | |
| | | | |
| | | | |
| | | | |

# STAKEHOLDER QUESTIONS

**LISTENING**

## Goal
Identify evidence needed to respond convincingly to stakeholder questions.

## Why
To respond to stakeholder questions, librarians need to provide supporting evidence.

## Directions
1. Consider typical stakeholder questions; add any that are missing. What do they care about? What concerns them?
2. Draft possible librarian responses to these questions that will achieve the desired stakeholder reaction.
3. Brainstorm evidence librarians need to support their responses to stakeholder questions.
4. Determine whether or not this evidence is currently available.
5. Engage the **T3** process.

## Suggested Reading
Oakleaf, Megan. *The Value of Academic Libraries: A Comprehensive Research Review and Report*. Chicago: ACRL, 2010. 26–30, 94.

## See Also
Activity #2: Stakeholders as the Heart of the Institution

 Seek first to understand, then to be understood."
—STEPHEN COVEY

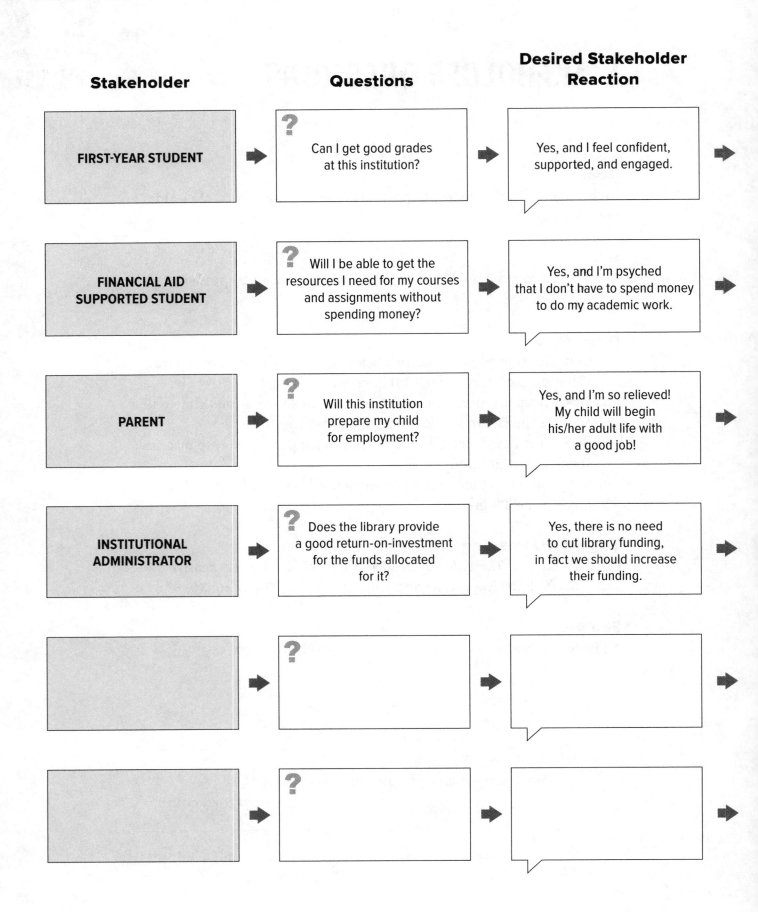

**Stakeholder** | **Questions** | **Desired Stakeholder Reaction**

FIRST-YEAR STUDENT → ? Can I get good grades at this institution? → Yes, and I feel confident, supported, and engaged. →

FINANCIAL AID SUPPORTED STUDENT → ? Will I be able to get the resources I need for my courses and assignments without spending money? → Yes, and I'm psyched that I don't have to spend money to do my academic work. →

PARENT → ? Will this institution prepare my child for employment? → Yes, and I'm so relieved! My child will begin his/her adult life with a good job! →

INSTITUTIONAL ADMINISTRATOR → ? Does the library provide a good return-on-investment for the funds allocated for it? → Yes, there is no need to cut library funding, in fact we should increase their funding. →

## Possible Library Responses to Achieve Reaction

## Evidence to Support Response

Librarians help you successfully define your information needs, then locate, evaluate, and use that information to do well on your assignments.

Do we currently have this evidence? ☐ YES ☐ NO

Librarians help you locate copies of textbooks and reserve readings. The databases supply articles and we'll ILL you what we don't have on site. You don't have to pay for a thing.

Do we currently have this evidence? ☐ YES ☐ NO

Librarians help students learn the skills employers seek: problem solving, critical thinking, creative inquiry, etc.

Do we currently have this evidence? ☐ YES ☐ NO

Librarians are excellent stewards of the resources they receive. We maximize benefits and minimize costs. We support faculty grant seeking, keep students retained, and seek out our own donors.

Do we currently have this evidence? ☐ YES ☐ NO

Do we currently have this evidence? ☐ YES ☐ NO

Do we currently have this evidence? ☐ YES ☐ NO

**THINK**   How did this activity make me feel?

_____

_____

What questions do I have?

_____

_____

What do I want to learn more about?

_____

_____

What innovative ideas have emerged?

_____

_____

**TALK**    What does this mean for my library? For me, as a librarian?

_____

_____

What do we need to do differently, as a library?

_____

_____

What does this make me want to continue to do, do better, or do differently, as a librarian?

_____

_____

**TARGET**

| Action | Timeframe | Responsible Parties | Follow-Up |
|---|---|---|---|
| **Options to Consider**<br>• Contact colleague<br>• Make decision<br>• Take action<br>• Ask question<br>• Get evidence/data | **When to Do It**<br>• Today<br>• This week<br>• This month<br>• This semester<br>• This year<br>• 2-3 year plan | **Who to Involve**<br>• Students<br>• Staff<br>• Librarians<br>• Administrators<br>• Faculty | **What to Do Next**<br>After I complete this action, what's the next step? |
|  |  |  |  |
|  |  |  |  |
|  |  |  |  |
|  |  |  |  |
|  |  |  |  |

# STAKEHOLDER CARD SORT

## Goal

Elicit stakeholder beliefs about the relative importance of institutional focus areas.

## Why

To assign institutional focus areas appropriate levels of attention, librarians need to query stakeholders about their perceptions of the relative importance of these focus areas.

## Directions

1. Identify a number of stakeholders.
2. Consider the institutional focus areas listed on the cards and in the chart. Are all of your institutional focus areas included? Cross out focus areas that do not apply; add any that are missing.
3. Photocopy and cut the institutional focus area cards apart.
4. Give the "deck" of institutional focus area cards to a stakeholder.
5. Ask the stakeholder to remove from the deck any cards with focus areas that are not important at your institution (or to him/her personally).
6. Ask the stakeholder to arrange the remaining cards in order of institutional (or personal) importance, with the most important focus area on top and the least important at the bottom of the deck.
7. Enter the numerical score for each focus area in the chart, with 1=least important. Record a zero for any card removed from the deck.
8. Repeat steps 4–7 with other stakeholders.
9. After recording all stakeholder responses, sum the scores given for each institutional focus area. Optional: Average the scores by dividing by the total number of stakeholders.
10. Consider the institutional focus areas that received the highest scores and those that received the lowest.
11. Engage the **T3** process.

## Suggested Reading

Oakleaf, Megan. *The Value of Academic Libraries: A Comprehensive Research Review and Report.*
   Chicago: ACRL, 2010. 26–30.

## See Also

Activity #1: Institutional Focus Areas
Activity #2: Stakeholders as the Heart of the Institution

## Stakeholder Card Sort

| | |
|---|---|
| Student Recruitment, Enrollment | Institutional Affordability |
| Student Retention, Completion, Graduation | Institutional Efficiencies |
| Student Career Success | Institutional Accreditation, Program Review |
| Student GPA, Test Achievement | Institutional Brand |
| Student Learning Outcomes | Institutional Athletics |
| Student Experience, Engagement | Institutional Development, Funding, Endowments |
| Student-Faculty Academic Rapport | Local, Global Workforce Development |
| Alumni Lifelong Learning | Local, Global Economic Growth |
| Faculty Recruitment, Tenure, Promotion | Local, Global Engagement, Community-Building, Social Inclusion |
| Faculty Teaching | |
| Faculty Teaching | |
| Faculty Research Productivity | |
| Faculty Grant Seeking | |
| Faculty Patents, Technology Transfer | |
| Faculty Innovation, Entrepreneurship | |
| Institutional Prestige | |

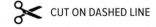 CUT ON DASHED LINE

| INSTITUTIONAL FOCUS AREAS | Stakeholder Group/Name: | Stakeholder Group/Name: | Stakeholder Group/Name | Stakeholder Group/Name | Stakeholder Group/Name | Stakeholder Group/Name | Stakeholder Group/Name | Stakeholder Group/Name | Stakeholder Group/Name | SUMMED SCORE | AVERAGE SCORE |
|---|---|---|---|---|---|---|---|---|---|---|---|
| Student Recruitment, Enrollment | | | | | | | | | | | |
| Student Retention, Completion, Graduation | | | | | | | | | | | |
| Student Career Success | | | | | | | | | | | |
| Student GPA, Test Achievement | | | | | | | | | | | |
| Student Learning Outcomes | | | | | | | | | | | |
| Student Experience, Engagement | | | | | | | | | | | |
| Student-Faculty Academic Rapport | | | | | | | | | | | |
| Alumni Lifelong Learning | | | | | | | | | | | |
| Faculty Recruitment, Tenure, Promotion | | | | | | | | | | | |
| Faculty Teaching | | | | | | | | | | | |
| Faculty Service | | | | | | | | | | | |
| Faculty Research Productivity | | | | | | | | | | | |
| Faculty Grant Seeking | | | | | | | | | | | |
| Faculty Patents, Technology Transfer | | | | | | | | | | | |
| Faculty Innovation, Entrepreneurship | | | | | | | | | | | |
| Institutional Prestige | | | | | | | | | | | |
| Institutional Affordability | | | | | | | | | | | |
| Institutional Efficiencies | | | | | | | | | | | |
| Institutional Accreditation, Program Review | | | | | | | | | | | |
| Institutional Brand | | | | | | | | | | | |
| Institutional Athletics | | | | | | | | | | | |
| Institutional Development, Funding, Endowments | | | | | | | | | | | |
| Local, Global Workforce Development | | | | | | | | | | | |
| Local, Global Economic Growth | | | | | | | | | | | |
| Local, Global Engagement, Community-Building, Social Inclusion | | | | | | | | | | | |
| Other: | | | | | | | | | | | |
| Other: | | | | | | | | | | | |
| Other: | | | | | | | | | | | |
| Other: | | | | | | | | | | | |

**THINK**

How did this activity make me feel?

_____

_____

What questions do I have?

_____

_____

What do I want to learn more about?

_____

_____

What innovative ideas have emerged?

_____

_____

**TALK**

What does this mean for my library? For me, as a librarian?

_____

_____

What do we need to do differently, as a library?

_____

_____

What does this make me want to continue to do, do better, or do differently, as a librarian?

_____

_____

**TARGET**

| Action | Timeframe | Responsible Parties | Follow-Up |
|---|---|---|---|
| **Options to Consider**<br>• Contact colleague<br>• Make decision<br>• Take action<br>• Ask question<br>• Get evidence/data | **When to Do It**<br>• Today<br>• This week<br>• This month<br>• This semester<br>• This year<br>• 2-3 year plan | **Who to Involve**<br>• Students<br>• Staff<br>• Librarians<br>• Administrators<br>• Faculty | **What to Do Next**<br>After I complete this action, what's the next step? |
|  |  |  |  |
|  |  |  |  |
|  |  |  |  |
|  |  |  |  |
|  |  |  |  |

**ACTIVITY #6**

# STAKEHOLDER HELP STUDY

## Goal

Elicit stakeholder beliefs about a recent library interaction and what that interaction has enabled them to do.

## Why

To articulate library contributions to institutional focus areas, librarians need to gather stakeholder perceptions of the impact of library interactions.

## Directions

1. Identify a number of stakeholders.
2. Using a survey or interview approach, deliver the following prompt: "Remember the last time the library or a librarian helped you. What help did you get? What did that help enable you to do?"
3. Record stakeholder responses.
4. Respond to the Reflection Questions.
5. Engage the **T3** process.

## Suggested Readings

Oakleaf, Megan, and Michelle Millet. "Help Yourself to Student Impact Data: Conducting a 'Help' Study to Explore Academic Library Value." ACRL Value of Academic Libraries Blog. http://www.acrl.ala.org/value/?p=285 (accessed May 15, 2012).

Whelan, Debra Lau. "13,000 Kids Can't Be Wrong." *School Library Journal*, 2004. http://www.schoollibraryjournal.com/article/CA377858.html (accessed May 10, 2010).

## See Also

Activity #2: Stakeholders as the Heart of the Institution

## Stakeholder Group

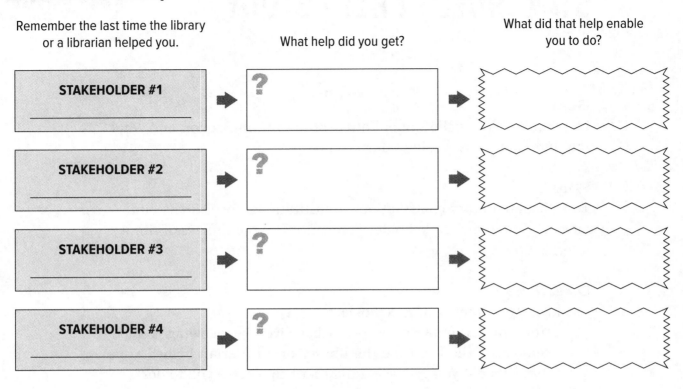

Remember the last time the library or a librarian helped you. | What help did you get? | What did that help enable you to do?

STAKEHOLDER #1

STAKEHOLDER #2

STAKEHOLDER #3

STAKEHOLDER #4

## Reflection Questions

1. What library services, expertise, and resources are mentioned most frequently?

_____

_____

2. Are these the services, expertise, and resources stakeholders "should" cite? Are there others about which stakeholders should be educated?

_____

_____

3. What were stakeholders enabled to do?

_____

_____

4. Who, within or outside the library, would be interested in the results of this activity?

_____

_____

**ENGAGE THE T3 PROCESS**

How did this activity make me feel?                                      **THINK**

_____

_____

What questions do I have?

_____

_____

What do I want to learn more about?

_____

_____

What innovative ideas have emerged?

_____

_____

What does this mean for my library? For me, as a librarian?             **TALK**

_____

_____

What do we need to do differently, as a library?

_____

_____

What does this make me want to continue to do, do better, or do differently, as a librarian?

_____

_____

| Action | Timeframe | Responsible Parties | Follow-Up |
|---|---|---|---|
| **Options to Consider**<br>• Contact colleague<br>• Make decision<br>• Take action<br>• Ask question<br>• Get evidence/data | **When to Do It**<br>• Today<br>• This week<br>• This month<br>• This semester<br>• This year<br>• 2-3 year plan | **Who to Involve**<br>• Students<br>• Staff<br>• Librarians<br>• Administrators<br>• Faculty | **What to Do Next**<br>After I complete this action, what's the next step? |
|  |  |  |  |
|  |  |  |  |
|  |  |  |  |
|  |  |  |  |
|  |  |  |  |

**TARGET**

ACTIVITY #7

# STAKEHOLDER VIEWS OF LIBRARY SERVICESCAPES

TAKING ACTION

## Goal
Assess the degree to which library service points communicate library contributions to institutional focus areas.

## Why
To articulate how library services support institutional focus areas, librarians need to envision how their services appear to stakeholders.

## Directions
1. Print and affix a photo of a library service point.
2. Choose two marker colors.
3. With the first color (insert color:_____), circle all items in the photo that communicate to stakeholders what they can do or how they can grow, change, or improve as a result of interacting with the service. Then, circle all items that show the service's contribution to institutional focus areas.
4. With the second color (insert color:_____), circle all items in the photo that do not communicate to stakeholders what they can do or how they can grow, change, or improve as a result of interacting with the service. Then, circle all items that do not show the service's contribution to institutional focus areas.
5. Respond to the Reflection Questions.
6. Engage the **T3** process.

## Suggested Reading
Oakleaf, Megan. *The Value of Academic Libraries: A Comprehensive Research Review and Report.* Chicago: ACRL, 2010. 26–30.

## See Also
Activity #1: Institutional Focus Areas
Activity #2: Stakeholders as the Heart of the Institution
Activity #26: Library Impact Map

## Stakeholder Views of Servicescapes

Affix photo of a library service point here.

## Reflection Questions

1. What does this service point enable stakeholders to do? How does it help them grow, change, or improve?

   _____

   _____

   _____

2. To what institutional focus areas does this service contribute?

   _____

   _____

   _____

3. List the items, circled in the first color, that clearly communicate to stakeholders what they can do or how they can grow, change, or improve as a result of interacting with this service, as well as the items that show the service's contribution to institutional focus areas.

   _____

   _____

   _____

4. What items could be added to the servicescape to communicate, demonstrate, and/or facilitate stakeholder abilities, growth, change, or improvement? Contribution to institutional focus areas?

   _____

   _____

   _____

5. List the items, circled in the second color, that do not clearly communicate to stakeholders what they can do or how they can grow, change, or improve as a result of interacting with this service, as well as the items that do not show the service's contribution to institutional focus areas.

   _____

   _____

   _____

6. What items could be removed from the servicescape?

   _____

   _____

   _____

**THINK**   How did this activity make me feel?

_____

_____

What questions do I have?

_____

_____

What do I want to learn more about?

_____

_____

What innovative ideas have emerged?

_____

_____

**TALK**   What does this mean for my library? For me, as a librarian?

_____

_____

What do we need to do differently, as a library?

_____

_____

What does this make me want to continue to do, do better, or do differently, as a librarian?

_____

_____

**TARGET**

| Action | Timeframe | Responsible Parties | Follow-Up |
|---|---|---|---|
| **Options to Consider**<br>• Contact colleague<br>• Make decision<br>• Take action<br>• Ask question<br>• Get evidence/data | **When to Do It**<br>• Today<br>• This week<br>• This month<br>• This semester<br>• This year<br>• 2-3 year plan | **Who to Involve**<br>• Students<br>• Staff<br>• Librarians<br>• Administrators<br>• Faculty | **What to Do Next**<br>After I complete this action, what's the next step? |
|  |  |  |  |
|  |  |  |  |
|  |  |  |  |
|  |  |  |  |
|  |  |  |  |

# INSTITUTIONAL COMMUNICATIONS AUDIT

## Goal
Identify the institutional focus areas of greatest importance to institutional leaders and administrators.

## Why
To target institutional focus areas of greatest strategic importance, librarians need to analyze the content of documents created and speeches given by institutional leaders and administrators.

## Directions
1. Identify several documents created or speeches given by institutional leaders and administrators. Documents may include institutional mission and vision statements, strategic plans, annual reports, alumni publications, press releases, etc. Speeches may include convocation and commencement addresses or presentations given at public events.
2. Read documents using critical and active reading techniques or listen to speeches using analysis strategies.
3. Respond to the Reflection Questions.
4. Engage the **T3** process.

## Suggested Reading
Oakleaf, Megan. *The Value of Academic Libraries: A Comprehensive Research Review and Report.* Chicago: ACRL, 2010. 26–30.

## See Also
Activity #1: Institutional Focus Areas

## Reading Documents

1. Consider what you want to learn from this document. Skim the Reflection Questions and brainstorm your own pre-reading questions.

   _____

   _____

2. As you read the document, highlight important ideas; create an outline, flowchart, or concept map; or make margin notes (i.e., questions after each section or an "X" where you disagree).

3. Describe what you read to a colleague.

## Reflection Questions

1. What institutional focus areas are revealed or detailed in this document/speech?

   _____

   _____

   _____

2. To which institutional focus areas mentioned in this document/speech does the library contribute?

   _____

   _____

   _____

3. What is this document/speech's message about library contributions to these institutional focus areas?

   _____

   _____

   _____

4. What inaccurate or limited conceptions about library contributions to institutional focus areas are contained in this document/speech?

   _____

   _____

   _____

5. How might librarians reshape or expand the role of the library in future documents/speeches?

   _____

   _____

   _____

## Listening to Speeches

**What I Want to Know:**

**Major Points Made:**
1.
2.
3.
4.
5.

**Anecdotes & Statistics Included:**

**Repeated Ideas, Themes, & Refrains:**

**Applause Lines:**

**What I Learned:**

**Terms & Phrases to Add to Shared Institutional Vocabulary:**

**THINK**

How did this activity make me feel?

_____

_____

What questions do I have?

_____

_____

What do I want to learn more about?

_____

_____

What innovative ideas have emerged?

_____

_____

**TALK**

What does this mean for my library? For me, as a librarian?

_____

_____

What do we need to do differently, as a library?

_____

_____

What does this make me want to continue to do, do better, or do differently, as a librarian?

_____

_____

**TARGET**

| Action | Timeframe | Responsible Parties | Follow-Up |
|---|---|---|---|
| **Options to Consider**<br>• Contact colleague<br>• Make decision<br>• Take action<br>• Ask question<br>• Get evidence/data | **When to Do It**<br>• Today<br>• This week<br>• This month<br>• This semester<br>• This year<br>• 2-3 year plan | **Who to Involve**<br>• Students<br>• Staff<br>• Librarians<br>• Administrators<br>• Faculty | **What to Do Next**<br>After I complete this action, what's the next step? |
|  |  |  |  |
|  |  |  |  |
|  |  |  |  |
|  |  |  |  |
|  |  |  |  |

# INSTITUTIONAL PROGRAM REVIEW AND ACCREDITATION AUDIT

## Goal
Connect library services, expertise, and resources with program review and accreditation.

## Why
To maximize library contributions to program review and accreditation, librarians need to determine ways in which they can generate, supply, and integrate relevant library evidence/data into both processes.

## Directions
1. Consider your institution's program review and accreditation processes. Gather documents and identify responsible parties for both processes and query them if additional information is necessary.
2. Determine the role of library evidence/data in these processes and documents.
3. Brainstorm ways in which existing or new library evidence/data could be used in future program review and accreditation processes and documents.
4. Engage the **T3** process.

## Suggested Reading
Oakleaf, Megan. *The Value of Academic Libraries: A Comprehensive Research Review and Report.* Chicago: ACRL, 2010. 54–55, 94–98.

## Program Review

1. Who is responsible for program review at your institution?

   _____

   _____

2. What purposes does program review serve?

   _____

   _____

3. What are the major goals and outcomes of program review?

   _____

   _____

4. Who is the audience of program review processes and documents?

   _____

   _____

5. What timelines and schedules are followed?

   _____

   _____

6. What kinds of information are included in program review processes and documents?

   _____

   _____

## Program Review and the Library

7. What library evidence/data has been included in program review processes and documents?

   _____

   _____

8. How has this library evidence/data been used?

   _____

   _____

9. What library evidence/data could be included in program review processes and documents in the future?

   _____

   _____

10. How could this new library evidence/data be used?

   _____

   _____

## Accreditation

1. What accrediting organizations impact your institution? Regional? Professional?

   _____

   _____

2. What library and information literacy content is included in accreditation guidelines and standards?

   _____

   _____

3. What accreditation guidelines and standards include institutional focus areas to which the library contributes?

   _____

   _____

4. Who is responsible for accreditation at your institution?

   _____

   _____

5. What timelines and schedules are followed?

   _____

   _____

6. What kinds of information are included in accreditation processes and documents?

   _____

   _____

## Accreditation and the Library

7. What library evidence/data has been included in accreditation processes and documents?

   _____

   _____

8. How has this library evidence/data been used?

   _____

   _____

9. What library evidence/data could be included in accreditation processes and documents in the future?

   _____

   _____

10. How could this new library evidence/data be used?

   _____

   _____

**THINK**

How did this activity make me feel?

_____

_____

What questions do I have?

_____

_____

What do I want to learn more about?

_____

_____

What innovative ideas have emerged?

_____

_____

**TALK**

What does this mean for my library? For me, as a librarian?

_____

_____

What do we need to do differently, as a library?

_____

_____

What does this make me want to continue to do, do better, or do differently, as a librarian?

_____

_____

**TARGET**

| Action | Timeframe | Responsible Parties | Follow-Up |
|---|---|---|---|
| **Options to Consider**<br>• Contact colleague<br>• Make decision<br>• Take action<br>• Ask question<br>• Get evidence/data | **When to Do It**<br>• Today<br>• This week<br>• This month<br>• This semester<br>• This year<br>• 2-3 year plan | **Who to Involve**<br>• Students<br>• Staff<br>• Librarians<br>• Administrators<br>• Faculty | **What to Do Next**<br>After I complete this action, what's the next step? |
|  |  |  |  |
|  |  |  |  |
|  |  |  |  |
|  |  |  |  |
|  |  |  |  |

**ACTIVITY #10**

# INSTITUTIONAL LEARNING OUTCOME AUDIT

## Goal
Connect library and information literacy learning outcomes with other institutionally relevant learning outcomes.

## Why
To maximize library contributions to the institutional focus area of student learning, librarians need to align information literacy learning outcomes with the learning outcomes relevant to their institutions.

## Directions
1. Gather documents that list institutionally relevant learning outcomes (e.g., general education outcomes, department and program outcomes, outcomes included in regional and professional accreditation standards, etc.).
2. Identify information literacy content within institutionally relevant learning outcome documents.
3. Articulate your library's information literacy learning outcomes.
4. Align institutional learning outcomes with information literacy learning outcomes.
5. Respond to the Reflection Questions.
6. Engage the **T3** process.

## Suggested Readings
Oakleaf, Megan. *The Value of Academic Libraries: A Comprehensive Research Review and Report*. Chicago: ACRL, 2010. 37–45, 94.

Oakleaf, Megan. "Are They Learning? Are We? Learning and the Academic Library." *Library Quarterly*. 81(1). 2011. 61–82.

> 66 If outcomes are the priority, and outcomes are achieved, students (and parents and other constituents) will have abundant reasons to be satisfied. But if there are no clear outcomes . . . or if those outcomes are not produced, ultimately, no one will be satisfied."
>
> —RICHARD KEELING

1. Locate documents that list learning outcomes relevant to your institution.
   - ○ General education outcomes
   - ○ Department and program outcomes
   - ○ Outcomes identified by regional accreditors
   - ○ Outcomes identified by professional accreditors
   - ○ Other: _____
   - ○ Other: _____

2. Analyze all documents; highlight information literacy content. Look for terms including:
   - ○ Information literacy
   - ○ Inquiry
   - ○ Information skills
   - ○ Critical thinking
   - ○ Research skills
   - ○ Information problem solving
   - ○ Independent scholarship
   - ○ 21st century skills
   - ○ Independent research
   - ○ Lifelong learning

3. Identify your library's information literacy outcomes.

4. Develop a chart, map, or crosswalk aligning information literacy outcomes with institutional learning outcomes.

| Information Literacy Outcomes | Institutionally Relevant Learning Outcomes |
|---|---|
| Define an information need | |
| Locate information | |
| Evaluate information | |
| Use information | |

| Information Literacy Outcomes | Institutionally Relevant Learning Outcomes |
|---|---|
| Use information ethically and responsibly | |
| "Authority Is Constructed and Contextual" outcomes | |
| "Information Creation as a Process" outcomes | |
| "Information Has Value" outcomes | |
| "Research as Inquiry" outcomes | |
| "Scholarship as Conversation" outcomes | |
| "Searching as Strategic Exploration" outcomes | |

## Reflection Questions

1. How well do information literacy outcomes align with institutional outcomes? Where are linkages strong? Where do linkages need to be strengthened?

_____

_____

_____

2. How might shared outcomes be taught most effectively?

_____

_____

_____

3. What partnerships, resources, tools, or processes need to be developed?

_____

_____

_____

4. How might shared outcomes be assessed collaboratively?

_____

_____

_____

5. How might collaborative assessment evidence/data be analyzed?

_____

_____

_____

6. How might collaborative assessment results be communicated, disseminated, and used to "close the loop"?

_____

_____

_____

**ENGAGE THE T3 PROCESS**

How did this activity make me feel?                                          THINK

_____

_____

What questions do I have?

_____

_____

What do I want to learn more about?

_____

_____

What innovative ideas have emerged?

_____

_____

What does this mean for my library? For me, as a librarian?                  TALK

_____

_____

What do we need to do differently, as a library?

_____

_____

What does this make me want to continue to do, do better, or do differently, as a librarian?

_____

_____

TARGET

| Action | Timeframe | Responsible Parties | Follow-Up |
|---|---|---|---|
| **Options to Consider**<br>• Contact colleague<br>• Make decision<br>• Take action<br>• Ask question<br>• Get evidence/data | **When to Do It**<br>• Today<br>• This week<br>• This month<br>• This semester<br>• This year<br>• 2-3 year plan | **Who to Involve**<br>• Students<br>• Staff<br>• Librarians<br>• Administrators<br>• Faculty | **What to Do Next**<br>After I complete this action, what's the next step? |
|  |  |  |  |
|  |  |  |  |
|  |  |  |  |
|  |  |  |  |
|  |  |  |  |

# HIGHER EDUCATION ASSESSMENT INITIATIVE AUDIT

## Goal
Identify higher education assessment initiatives and organizations that parallel institutional focus areas and anticipate intersections between higher education and library assessment activities.

## Why
To connect library contributions to institutional focus areas, librarians need to identify overarching assessment initiatives and organizations impacting all of higher education and align library services, expertise, and resources with these efforts.

## Directions
1. Consider higher education assessment initiatives and organizations in the left column; add any that are missing.
2. Research each initiative or organization; determine its intent, mission, goals, etc.
3. Determine your institution's level of involvement in each initiative or organization.
4. Brainstorm ways in which the library does or could contribute to your institution's involvement in each initiative or organization.
5. Engage the **T3** process.

## Suggested Reading
Oakleaf, Megan. *The Value of Academic Libraries: A Comprehensive Research Review and Report*. Chicago: ACRL, 2010. 26–28, 97–98.

| Higher Education Initiative | Initiative Intent |
| --- | --- |
| Voluntary System of Accountability | |
| Voluntary Framework of Accountability | |
| Achieving the Dream | |
| University and College Accountability Network | |
| National Institute for Learning Outcomes Assessment | |
| Assessment of Higher Education Learning Outcomes | |
| Liberal Education and America's Promise | |
| Association for the Assessment of Learning in Higher Education | |
| New Leadership Alliance | |
| Bologna Process | |
| Tuning USA | |
| Other: | |
| Other: | |
| Other: | |

| Institutional Involvement with Initiative | Library Contributions to Institutional Involvement with Initiative |
|---|---|
| | |
| | |
| | |
| | |
| | |
| | |
| | |
| | |
| | |
| | |
| | |
| | |
| | |

**THINK**        How did this activity make me feel?
_____
_____

What questions do I have?
_____
_____

What do I want to learn more about?
_____
_____

What innovative ideas have emerged?
_____
_____

**TALK**         What does this mean for my library? For me, as a librarian?
_____
_____

What do we need to do differently, as a library?
_____
_____

What does this make me want to continue to do, do better, or do differently, as a librarian?
_____
_____

**TARGET**

| Action | Timeframe | Responsible Parties | Follow-Up |
|---|---|---|---|
| **Options to Consider**<br>• Contact colleague<br>• Make decision<br>• Take action<br>• Ask question<br>• Get evidence/data | **When to Do It**<br>• Today<br>• This week<br>• This month<br>• This semester<br>• This year<br>• 2-3 year plan | **Who to Involve**<br>• Students<br>• Staff<br>• Librarians<br>• Administrators<br>• Faculty | **What to Do Next**<br>After I complete this action, what's the next step? |
|  |  |  |  |
|  |  |  |  |
|  |  |  |  |
|  |  |  |  |
|  |  |  |  |

ACTIVITY #12

# LIBRARY DATA AUDIT

**GETTING ORGANIZED**

## Goal

Examine the attributes of existing or potential library data.

## Why

To determine the utility of existing data or decide to elicit new or different data, librarians need to assess the characteristics of currently available and/or data to collect in the future.

## Directions

1. Consider the data elements currently collected by the library.
2. Optional: Consider the data elements the library may collect in the future.
3. Enter each data element in the left column.
4. For each data element, check the appropriate boxes to indicate the type of data, considerations for accessing the data, attributes that impact the data's relevance, potential venues for data dissemination, and other data characteristics.
5. Consider for each data element: Is this a data element that should represent the library? Is this a data element that should be used to judge the library?
6. Engage the **T3** process.

> ❝ The data we collect represents what we value about ourselves and determines how others will judge us. Given the data we currently collect, are we prepared to live with that?"
>
> —MEGAN OAKLEAF

49

## Library Data Audit

| DATA ELEMENTS (currently collected or may be collected in the future) | TYPE | | | | | | | | | | | | ACCESS | | | | | | | | | RELEVANCE | | | | | | |
|---|---|---|---|---|---|---|---|---|---|---|---|---|---|---|---|---|---|---|---|---|---|---|---|---|---|---|---|---|
| | Input | Output | Outcome | Librarian time/effort | Use | Satisfaction | Service quality | Group-level | Individual-level | Other: | Other: | Other: | Available/not yet available | In library information systems | In vendor information systems | In student information systems | In institutional information systems | In state/national information systems | Other: | Other: | Other: | Meaningful to stakeholders | Formatted according to stakeholder preferences | Useful to library management of services, expertise, & resources | Answers open questions | Enables decision making | Enables resource allocations | Enables actions |
| | | | | | | | | | | | | | | | | | | | | | | | | | | | | |
| | | | | | | | | | | | | | | | | | | | | | | | | | | | | |
| | | | | | | | | | | | | | | | | | | | | | | | | | | | | |
| | | | | | | | | | | | | | | | | | | | | | | | | | | | | |
| | | | | | | | | | | | | | | | | | | | | | | | | | | | | |
| | | | | | | | | | | | | | | | | | | | | | | | | | | | | |
| | | | | | | | | | | | | | | | | | | | | | | | | | | | | |
| | | | | | | | | | | | | | | | | | | | | | | | | | | | | |
| | | | | | | | | | | | | | | | | | | | | | | | | | | | | |
| | | | | | | | | | | | | | | | | | | | | | | | | | | | | |
| | | | | | | | | | | | | | | | | | | | | | | | | | | | | |
| | | | | | | | | | | | | | | | | | | | | | | | | | | | | |
| | | | | | | | | | | | | | | | | | | | | | | | | | | | | |
| | | | | | | | | | | | | | | | | | | | | | | | | | | | | |
| | | | | | | | | | | | | | | | | | | | | | | | | | | | | |
| | | | | | | | | | | | | | | | | | | | | | | | | | | | | |

What data do we need, but do not have?

| RELEVANCE | | | | | | | DISSEMINATION | | | | | | | | | | | | OTHER CONSIDERATIONS | | | | | | | |
|---|---|---|---|---|---|---|---|---|---|---|---|---|---|---|---|---|---|---|---|---|---|---|---|---|---|---|
| Worth sharing | Related to instructional focus areas | Related to educational/professional standards | Related to Value of Academic Libraries research agenda | Other: | Other: | Other: | In library communications | In assessment planning documents | In strategic planning documents | In program review/accreditation documents | In campus presentations | In conference presentations | In campus publications | In scholarly publications | Other: | Other: | Other: | IRB required | Method/tool used to collect | Costs | Required by library professional association | | | Other: | Other: | Other: | Ultimately, is this a data element that represents the library as we would like to be represented? As we would like to be judged? |
| | | | | | | | | | | | | | | | | | | | | | | | | | | | |
| | | | | | | | | | | | | | | | | | | | | | | | | | | | |
| | | | | | | | | | | | | | | | | | | | | | | | | | | | |
| | | | | | | | | | | | | | | | | | | | | | | | | | | | |
| | | | | | | | | | | | | | | | | | | | | | | | | | | | |
| | | | | | | | | | | | | | | | | | | | | | | | | | | | |
| | | | | | | | | | | | | | | | | | | | | | | | | | | | |
| | | | | | | | | | | | | | | | | | | | | | | | | | | | |
| | | | | | | | | | | | | | | | | | | | | | | | | | | | |
| | | | | | | | | | | | | | | | | | | | | | | | | | | | |
| | | | | | | | | | | | | | | | | | | | | | | | | | | | |
| | | | | | | | | | | | | | | | | | | | | | | | | | | | |
| | | | | | | | | | | | | | | | | | | | | | | | | | | | |
| | | | | | | | | | | | | | | | | | | | | | | | | | | | |
| | | | | | | | | | | | | | | | | | | | | | | | | | | | |
| | | | | | | | | | | | | | | | | | | | | | | | | | | | |
| | | | | | | | | | | | | | | | | | | | | | | | | | | | |
| | | | | | | | | | | | | | | | | | | | | | | | | | | | |
| | | | | | | | | | | | | | | | | | | | | | | | | | | | |

**THINK**

How did this activity make me feel?

_____

_____

What questions do I have?

_____

_____

What do I want to learn more about?

_____

_____

What innovative ideas have emerged?

_____

_____

**TALK**

What does this mean for my library? For me, as a librarian?

_____

_____

What do we need to do differently, as a library?

_____

_____

What does this make me want to continue to do, do better, or do differently, as a librarian?

_____

_____

**TARGET**

| Action | Timeframe | Responsible Parties | Follow-Up |
|---|---|---|---|
| **Options to Consider**<br>• Contact colleague<br>• Make decision<br>• Take action<br>• Ask question<br>• Get evidence/data | **When to Do It**<br>• Today<br>• This week<br>• This month<br>• This semester<br>• This year<br>• 2-3 year plan | **Who to Involve**<br>• Students<br>• Staff<br>• Librarians<br>• Administrators<br>• Faculty | **What to Do Next**<br>After I complete this action, what's the next step? |
|  |  |  |  |
|  |  |  |  |
|  |  |  |  |
|  |  |  |  |
|  |  |  |  |

**ACTIVITY #13**

# TIME AUDIT

## Goal
Examine the time spent, or not spent, contributing to institutional focus areas.

## Why
To increase their impact on institutional focus areas, librarians need to consider the degree to which their work activities reflect an institutional emphasis.

## Directions
1. For one week, plot your work activities on the schedule. Include group meetings, individual work tasks, important calls or emails, etc.
2. At the end of the week, choose two highlighter colors. With the first color (insert color:_____), highlight all activities directly related to institutional focus areas, such as:

   ○ Student Recruitment, Enrollment
   ○ Student Retention, Completion, Graduation
   ○ Student Career Success
   ○ Student GPA, Test Achievement
   ○ Student Learning Outcomes
   ○ Student Experience, Engagement
   ○ Student-Faculty Academic Rapport
   ○ Alumni Lifelong Learning
   ○ Faculty Recruitment, Tenure, Promotion
   ○ Faculty Teaching
   ○ Faculty Service
   ○ Faculty Research Productivity
   ○ Faculty Grant Seeking
   ○ Faculty Patents, Technology Transfer
   ○ Faculty Innovation, Entrepreneurship
   ○ Institutional Prestige
   ○ Institutional Affordability
   ○ Institutional Efficiencies

- ○ Institutional Accreditation, Program Review
- ○ Institutional Brand
- ○ Institutional Athletics
- ○ Institutional Development, Funding, Endowments
- ○ Local, Global Workforce Development
- ○ Local, Global Economic Growth
- ○ Local, Global Engagement, Community-Building, Social Inclusion

3. With the second color (insert color:_____), highlight all activities that are not directly related to institutional focus.
4. Respond to the Reflection Questions.
5. Engage the **T3** process.

**See Also**
Activity #1: Institutional Focus Areas

# Time Audit

| | MONDAY | TUESDAY | WEDNESDAY | THURSDAY | FRIDAY | Reflection Questions |
|---|---|---|---|---|---|---|
| 8:00 | | | | | | What institutional focus areas did I contribute to this week? What exactly did I do to contribute to them? Did I make them my top priority? |
| 8:30 | | | | | | _____ |
| 9:00 | | | | | | _____ |
| 9:30 | | | | | | _____ |
| 10:00 | | | | | | _____ |
| 10:30 | | | | | | _____ |
| 11:00 | | | | | | _____ |
| 11:30 | | | | | | What am I doing that is less important than contributing to institutional focus areas? |
| 12:00 | | | | | | _____ |
| 12:30 | | | | | | _____ |
| 1:00 | | | | | | _____ |
| 1:30 | | | | | | _____ |
| 2:00 | | | | | | _____ |
| 2:30 | | | | | | How can I maximize the time and effort I contribute to institutional focus areas? What can I start doing? Stop doing? |
| 3:00 | | | | | | _____ |
| 3:30 | | | | | | _____ |
| 4:00 | | | | | | _____ |
| 4:30 | | | | | | _____ |
| 5:00 | | | | | | _____ |

**THINK**

How did this activity make me feel?

_____

_____

What questions do I have?

_____

_____

What do I want to learn more about?

_____

_____

What innovative ideas have emerged?

_____

_____

**TALK**

What does this mean for my library? For me, as a librarian?

_____

_____

What do we need to do differently, as a library?

_____

_____

What does this make me want to continue to do, do better, or do differently, as a librarian?

_____

_____

**TARGET**

| Action | Timeframe | Responsible Parties | Follow-Up |
|---|---|---|---|
| **Options to Consider** <br> • Contact colleague <br> • Make decision <br> • Take action <br> • Ask question <br> • Get evidence/data | **When to Do It** <br> • Today <br> • This week <br> • This month <br> • This semester <br> • This year <br> • 2-3 year plan | **Who to Involve** <br> • Students <br> • Staff <br> • Librarians <br> • Administrators <br> • Faculty | **What to Do Next** <br> After I complete this action, what's the next step? |
|  |  |  |  |
|  |  |  |  |
|  |  |  |  |
|  |  |  |  |
|  |  |  |  |

ACTIVITY #14
# SELF AUDIT

**GETTING ORGANIZED**

### Goal
Reflect on the role of the individual librarian in contributing to institutional focus areas.

### Why
To link their individual work to institutional focus areas, librarians need to examine their job duties, tasks, and responsibilities, as well as their role in evidence collection and establishing partnerships.

### Directions
1. Respond to the Reflection Questions.
2. Engage the **T3** process.

### Suggested Reading
Keeling, Richard P. *Learning Reconsidered 2: Implementing a Campus-Wide Focus on the Student Experience.* American College Personnel Association, 2006.

### See Also
Activity #1: Institutional Focus Areas
Activity #2: Stakeholders as the Heart of the Institution
Activity #13: Time Audit

> ❝ Why are you making all this effort? Because you believe that libraries enable people to do things and that these things make a difference. You want to find out what difference we helped people make, and therefore, what difference **we** make."
>
> —MEGAN OAKLEAF

## Reflection Questions

1. Consider your daily job tasks, duties, and responsibilities. What impact do they have on stakeholders? What does your job enable them to do? How does it help them grow, change, or improve?

   _____

   _____

   _____

   _____

2. Consider the tasks, duties, and responsibilities you wish were a part of your job if you had more time, staff, support, etc. What impact could they have on stakeholders? What could your job enable them to do? How could it help them grow, change, or improve?

   _____

   _____

   _____

   _____

3. To what institutional focus areas does your job contribute?

   _____

   _____

   _____

   _____

4. What evidence exists to show the contribution of your job to these institutional focus areas? What does the evidence say? Not say?

   _____

   _____

   _____

   _____

5. What additional evidence could you gather to show the contribution of your job to institutional focus areas?

   _____

   _____

   _____

   _____

6. Imagine you had that evidence in hand. How would you use it to make decisions and take actions?

   _____

   _____

   _____

   _____

7. What collaborative partnerships do you need to establish or reinforce in order to support your contribution to institutional focus areas?

   _____

   _____

   _____

   _____

8. What challenges do you face in beginning, continuing, or expanding your contribution to institutional focus areas?

   _____

   _____

   _____

   _____

9. How could you overcome these challenges?

   _____

   _____

   _____

   _____

10. What job tasks, duties, and responsibilities do you do that are not contributing to institutional focus areas?

   _____

   _____

   _____

   _____

**THINK**

How did this activity make me feel?

_____

_____

What questions do I have?

_____

_____

What do I want to learn more about?

_____

_____

What innovative ideas have emerged?

_____

_____

**TALK**

What does this mean for my library? For me, as a librarian?

_____

_____

What do we need to do differently, as a library?

_____

_____

What does this make me want to continue to do, do better, or do differently, as a librarian?

_____

_____

**TARGET**

| Action | Timeframe | Responsible Parties | Follow-Up |
|---|---|---|---|
| **Options to Consider**<br>• Contact colleague<br>• Make decision<br>• Take action<br>• Ask question<br>• Get evidence/data | **When to Do It**<br>• Today<br>• This week<br>• This month<br>• This semester<br>• This year<br>• 2-3 year plan | **Who to Involve**<br>• Students<br>• Staff<br>• Librarians<br>• Administrators<br>• Faculty | **What to Do Next**<br>After I complete this action, what's the next step? |
| | | | |
| | | | |
| | | | |
| | | | |
| | | | |

ACTIVITY #15
# JOB TASK AUDIT

GETTING ORGANIZED

## Goal

Determine the degree to which existing job duties, tasks, and responsibilities contribute to institutional focus areas.

## Why

To establish linkages between job duties, tasks, and responsibilities and institutional focus areas, librarians need to analyze the jobs of individuals and groups in the library.

## Directions

1. Respond to questions #1–5 as an individual.
2. Optional: If job duties, tasks, and responsibilities are completed by larger groups (e.g., units, committees, or departments), ask all members of the group to respond to questions #1–5 independently. Then, as a group, discuss and respond to questions #6–10.
3. Engage the **T3** process.

## See Also

Activity #1: Institutional Focus Areas
Activity #2: Stakeholders as the Heart of the Institution

## As an Individual

1. What are your job duties, tasks, or responsibilities?

2. For each response to question #1, what institutional focus area does that duty, task, or responsibility contribute to? If none, write "none."

_____ ➡ _____

_____ ➡ _____

_____ ➡ _____

_____ ➡ _____

_____ ➡ _____

_____ ➡ _____

3. For each completed response to question #2, explain how that duty, task, or responsibility contributes to the stated institutional focus area, as well as what evidence of the contribution exists.

_____

_____

_____

4. For each "none" response to question #2, explain why that duty, task, or responsibility is (or is not) important, considering its lack of contribution to institutional focus areas. (Ponder: Is it a duty, task, or responsibility that enables a service or resource that in turn contributes to an institutional focus area? If so, revise your response to question #2.)

_____

_____

_____

5. Reflect on your response to question #4. Are there any duties, tasks, or responsibilities that you could stop doing?

_____

_____

_____

## As a Group

6. As a group (e.g., unit, committee, or department), which of your shared duties, tasks, or responsibilities make the greatest or clearest contribution to institutional focus areas?

   _____

   _____

   _____

7. As a group, what could you do to articulate the contribution of your shared duties, tasks, or responsibilities within the library?

   _____

   _____

   _____

8. As a group, what could you do to articulate the contribution of your shared duties, tasks, or responsibilities to stakeholders?

   _____

   _____

   _____

9. As a group, which of your shared duties, tasks, or responsibilities make the least contribution to institutional focus areas?

   _____

   _____

   _____

10. As a group, what could you stop doing?

   _____

   _____

   _____

**THINK**

How did this activity make me feel?

_____

_____

What questions do I have?

_____

_____

What do I want to learn more about?

_____

_____

What innovative ideas have emerged?

_____

_____

**TALK**

What does this mean for my library? For me, as a librarian?

_____

_____

What do we need to do differently, as a library?

_____

_____

What does this make me want to continue to do, do better, or do differently, as a librarian?

_____

_____

**TARGET**

| Action | Timeframe | Responsible Parties | Follow-Up |
|---|---|---|---|
| **Options to Consider**<br>• Contact colleague<br>• Make decision<br>• Take action<br>• Ask question<br>• Get evidence/data | **When to Do It**<br>• Today<br>• This week<br>• This month<br>• This semester<br>• This year<br>• 2-3 year plan | **Who to Involve**<br>• Students<br>• Staff<br>• Librarians<br>• Administrators<br>• Faculty | **What to Do Next**<br>After I complete this action, what's the next step? |
|  |  |  |  |
|  |  |  |  |
|  |  |  |  |
|  |  |  |  |
|  |  |  |  |

# JOB DESCRIPTION AUDIT

## Goal
Analyze the degree to which library positions include duties, tasks, and responsibilities that contribute to institutional focus areas.

## Why
To align library positions with institutional focus areas, librarians need to examine existing and proposed position descriptions to ensure that job duties, tasks, and responsibilities reflect appropriate emphasis on institutional focus areas.

## Directions
1. Select and affix an existing or proposed library position description.
2. Choose two highlighter colors. With the first color (insert color: _____), highlight all job duties, tasks, or responsibilities that contribute to institutional focus areas.
3. With the second highlighter color, (insert color:_____), highlight all job duties, tasks, or responsibilities that do not contribute to institutional focus areas.
4. Respond to the Reflection Questions.
5. Engage the **T3** process.

## Suggested Reading
Oakleaf, Megan and Scott Walter. "Recruitment for Results: Assessment Skills and the Academic Job Market." *Proceedings of the Library Assessment Conference.* Baltimore, MD: Association of Research Libraries. 2010.

## See Also
Activity #1: Institutional Focus Areas
Activity #19: Skill Audit

Affix job description here.

## Reflection Questions

1. Does the balance between the first and second colors seem appropriate? Why or why not?

   _____

   _____

   _____

2. Consider the job duties, tasks, or responsibilities highlighted in the first color. To what institutional focus areas do these duties, tasks, or responsibilities contribute?

   _____

   _____

3. What other institutional focus areas should this position contribute to? How might the position description be rewritten to include those focus areas?

   _____

   _____

   _____

4. Does this position description clearly articulate the assessment skills and tasks required to help demonstrate the contribution of this position to institutional focus areas? How might the position description be rewritten to include these skills and tasks?

   _____

   _____

   _____

5. For proposed positions, does this description include a list of qualifications that will ensure the new hire will be prepared to undertake all the listed job duties, tasks, or responsibilities? How might the position desciption be rewritten to include these qualifications?

   _____

   _____

   _____

**THINK**

How did this activity make me feel?

_____

_____

What questions do I have?

_____

_____

What do I want to learn more about?

_____

_____

What innovative ideas have emerged?

_____

_____

**TALK**

What does this mean for my library? For me, as a librarian?

_____

_____

What do we need to do differently, as a library?

_____

_____

What does this make me want to continue to do, do better, or do differently, as a librarian?

_____

_____

**TARGET**

| Action | Timeframe | Responsible Parties | Follow-Up |
|---|---|---|---|
| **Options to Consider**<br>• Contact colleague<br>• Make decision<br>• Take action<br>• Ask question<br>• Get evidence/data | **When to Do It**<br>• Today<br>• This week<br>• This month<br>• This semester<br>• This year<br>• 2-3 year plan | **Who to Involve**<br>• Students<br>• Staff<br>• Librarians<br>• Administrators<br>• Faculty | **What to Do Next**<br>After I complete this action, what's the next step? |
|  |  |  |  |
|  |  |  |  |
|  |  |  |  |
|  |  |  |  |
|  |  |  |  |

# COMMITTEE AUDIT

## Goal
Determine the level of librarian integration into institution-level committees.

## Why
To fully engage in conversations surrounding institutional focus areas, librarians need to maximize their participation in institution-level committees.

## Directions
1. List institution-level committees in the left column.
2. For each committee, state whether or not a librarian is a committee member. If so, list his/her name. If not, list a librarian to seek committee membership and the procedures for doing so.
3. For each committee, determine the strategic goal of librarian inclusion on the committee, from both a library perspective as well as in the context of institutional focus areas.
4. Respond to the Reflection Questions.
5. Engage the **T3** process.

## See Also
Activity #1: Institutional Focus Areas

| Institution-Level Committees | Librarian Committee Member | Librarian's Strategic Goal as Committee Member | Librarian to Recommend for Future Committee Membership | Process for Pursuing Committee Membership |
|---|---|---|---|---|
| | | | | |
| | | | | |
| | | | | |
| | | | | |
| | | | | |
| | | | | |
| | | | | |
| | | | | |

## Reflection Questions

1. To what degree have librarians become integrated into institution-level committees? What committees do not currently benefit from librarian representation?

   _____

   _____

   _____

   _____

   _____

2. What strategic goals are librarians seeking to achieve through their membership on these committees (other than the achievement of committee charges)?

   _____

   _____

   _____

   _____

   _____

3. What contributions to institutional focus areas have librarians made as a consequence of their committee membership?

   _____

   _____

   _____

   _____

   _____

**THINK**

How did this activity make me feel?

_____

_____

What questions do I have?

_____

_____

What do I want to learn more about?

_____

_____

What innovative ideas have emerged?

_____

_____

**TALK**

What does this mean for my library? For me, as a librarian?

_____

_____

What do we need to do differently, as a library?

_____

_____

What does this make me want to continue to do, do better, or do differently, as a librarian?

_____

_____

**TARGET**

| Action | Timeframe | Responsible Parties | Follow-Up |
|---|---|---|---|
| **Options to Consider**<br>• Contact colleague<br>• Make decision<br>• Take action<br>• Ask question<br>• Get evidence/data | **When to Do It**<br>• Today<br>• This week<br>• This month<br>• This semester<br>• This year<br>• 2-3 year plan | **Who to Involve**<br>• Students<br>• Staff<br>• Librarians<br>• Administrators<br>• Faculty | **What to Do Next**<br>After I complete this action, what's the next step? |
|  |  |  |  |
|  |  |  |  |
|  |  |  |  |
|  |  |  |  |
|  |  |  |  |

# MANAGEMENT AUDIT

## Goal

Plan actions to support assessment best practices and anticipate "cause and effect" relationships between those practices and possible results.

## Why

To make intentional changes for improvement, librarians with supervisory, managerial, or administrative responsibilities need to select best practices in support of assessment activities and envision their consequences.

## Directions

1. As a librarian with supervisory, managerial, or administrative responsibilities, consider the list of best practices; add any that are missing.
2. Select best practices.
3. Brainstorm tasks to enact in support of each practice.
4. Predict the effect of each task.
5. Consider: Is the effect positive or negative? Why?
6. Decide: Is this a task to undertake?
7. Engage the **T3** process.

## Suggested Reading

Oakleaf, Megan. *The Value of Academic Libraries: A Comprehensive Research Review and Report.* Chicago: ACRL, 2010. 98–99.

**Best Practice**                                     **Action**

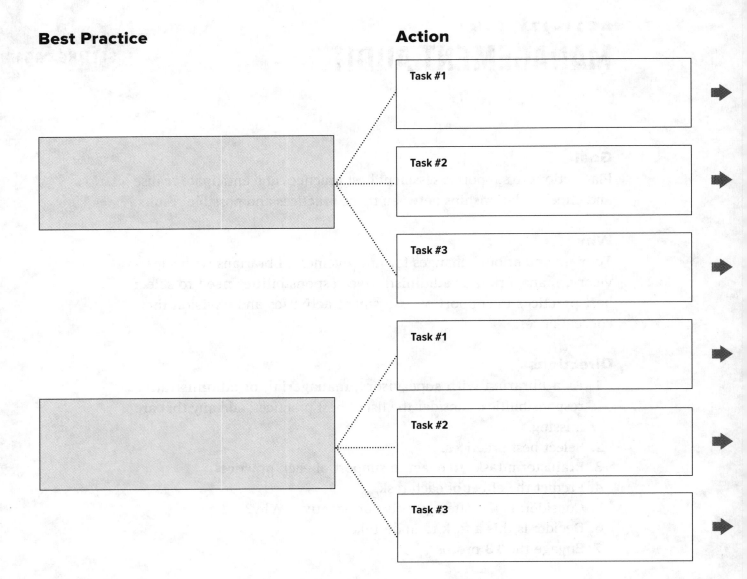

## Best Practices

- Tie library value/impact to institutional focus areas.
- Communicate assessment results to stakeholders.
- Model evidence-based decision-making.
- Dedicate personnel to assessment activities.
- Provide access to and support for assessment, professional development, and training.

- Integrate assessment into library and institutional strategic planning documents.
- Integrate assessment into library and institutional budget structures.
- Integrate assessment into library and institutional reward systems.
- Provide adequate resources (financial, time, personnel) for assessment activities.

## Expectation

| Anticipated Effect #1 |
| --- |

➡

| ○ Positive      Why?<br>○ Negative |
| --- |

| Anticipated Effect #2 |
| --- |

➡

| ○ Positive      Why?<br>○ Negative |
| --- |

| Anticipated Effect #3 |
| --- |

➡

| ○ Positive      Why?<br>○ Negative |
| --- |

| Anticipated Effect #1 |
| --- |

➡

| ○ Positive      Why?<br>○ Negative |
| --- |

| Anticipated Effect #2 |
| --- |

➡

| ○ Positive      Why?<br>○ Negative |
| --- |

| Anticipated Effect #3 |
| --- |

➡

| ○ Positive      Why?<br>○ Negative |
| --- |

## Reflection

- Communicate clear expectations about assessment roles and responsibilities.
- Reassign work tasks to "make room" for assessment as needed.
- Create confidence in assessment efforts.
- Encourage creative approaches to assessment.
- Accept that mistakes are a part of innovative change.

- Other:

    _____

    _____

- Other:

    _____

    _____

- Other:

    _____

    _____

**THINK**      How did this activity make me feel?

_____

_____

What questions do I have?

_____

_____

What do I want to learn more about?

_____

_____

What innovative ideas have emerged?

_____

_____

**TALK**       What does this mean for my library? For me, as a librarian?

_____

_____

What do we need to do differently, as a library?

_____

_____

What does this make me want to continue to do, do better, or do differently, as a librarian?

_____

_____

**TARGET**

| Action | Timeframe | Responsible Parties | Follow-Up |
|---|---|---|---|
| **Options to Consider**<br>• Contact colleague<br>• Make decision<br>• Take action<br>• Ask question<br>• Get evidence/data | **When to Do It**<br>• Today<br>• This week<br>• This month<br>• This semester<br>• This year<br>• 2-3 year plan | **Who to Involve**<br>• Students<br>• Staff<br>• Librarians<br>• Administrators<br>• Faculty | **What to Do Next**<br>After I complete this action, what's the next step? |
|  |  |  |  |
|  |  |  |  |
|  |  |  |  |
|  |  |  |  |
|  |  |  |  |

ACTIVITY #19
# SKILL AUDIT

## Goal
Identify acquired skills and diagnose skill gaps.

## Why
To design personal or library-wide professional development opportunities, librarians need to determine assessment learning needs.

## Directions
1. Consider the list of assessment skills; add any that are missing.
2. For each skill, indicate your level of knowledge or need for learning.
3. Reflect. For what skills do you need to seek professional development?
4. Reflect. Are there any skills that you could help others learn?
5. Engage the **T3** process.

## Suggested Reading
Oakleaf, Megan and Scott Walter. "Recruitment for Results: Assessment Skills and the Academic Job Market." *Proceedings of the Library Assessment Conference.* Baltimore, MD: Association of Research Libraries. 2010.

## See Also
Activity #20: Professional Development Plan

> **LEGEND**
>
> ⑤ Know enough to teach others.
>
> ④ Know enough to do my job.
>
> ③ Need to learn more; will seek professional development opportunities.
>
> ② Need to learn more; will not seek professional development opportunities at this time.
>
> ① Don't know if I know enough or if I need to learn more.

## Higher Education Context

○ Identify, describe, and participate in current issues related to higher education accountability. ⑤ ④ ③ ② ①

○ Identify, describe, and participate in current issues related to regional and professional accreditation. ⑤ ④ ③ ② ①

○ Identify, describe, and participate in current issues related to standards guiding higher education assessment. ⑤ ④ ③ ② ①

○ Identify, describe, and participate in current issues related to challenges confronting higher education assessment processes. ⑤ ④ ③ ② ①

○ Identify, describe, and participate in current issues related to multi-institution assessment initiatives. ⑤ ④ ③ ② ①

○ Other: _____ ⑤ ④ ③ ② ①

○ Other: _____ ⑤ ④ ③ ② ①

## Institutional Context

○ Frame and communicate library impact on institutional focus areas. ⑤ ④ ③ ② ①

○ Leverage centrality of library to "break institutional silos." ⑤ ④ ③ ② ①

○ Increase visibility of library within institution. ⑤ ④ ③ ② ①

○ Other: _____ ⑤ ④ ③ ② ①

○ Other: _____ ⑤ ④ ③ ② ①

## The Data

○ Identify data sources and describe data elements available in each source. ⑤ ④ ③ ② ①

○ Integrate library data with institution-level systems, including student information systems. ⑤ ④ ③ ② ①

○ Manage data sets using appropriate tools (e.g., assessment management systems). ⑤ ④ ③ ② ①

○ Define data needs.                                                           ⑤ ④ ③ ② ①
○ Analyze data using standard analysis tools (e.g., Excel, SPSS).              ⑤ ④ ③ ② ①
○ Interpret data.                                                              ⑤ ④ ③ ② ①
○ Triangulate data sources.                                                    ⑤ ④ ③ ② ①
○ Correlate data and explore potential causal relationships.                   ⑤ ④ ③ ② ①
○ Format data for multiple stakeholder needs.                                  ⑤ ④ ③ ② ①
○ Communicate data and data analysis decisions.                                ⑤ ④ ③ ② ①
○ Use data for decision-making and action-taking.                              ⑤ ④ ③ ② ①
○ Other: _____                      ⑤ ④ ③ ② ①
○ Other: _____                      ⑤ ④ ③ ② ①

## Collaboration

○ Determine key collaborative partners.                                        ⑤ ④ ③ ② ①
○ Approach and establish collaborative partnerships.                           ⑤ ④ ③ ② ①
○ Establish shared vocabulary.                                                 ⑤ ④ ③ ② ①
○ Develop and manage partnerships.                                             ⑤ ④ ③ ② ①
○ Other: _____                      ⑤ ④ ③ ② ①
○ Other: _____                      ⑤ ④ ③ ② ①

## Assessment

○ Define outcomes.                                                             ⑤ ④ ③ ② ①
○ Identify the purposes, values, or theories guiding assessment activities.    ⑤ ④ ③ ② ①
○ Link assessment activities to institutional and library planning documents.  ⑤ ④ ③ ② ①
○ Design assessment or research projects.                                      ⑤ ④ ③ ② ①
○ Secure resources for assessment activities.                                  ⑤ ④ ③ ② ①
○ Utilize project management strategies and tools.                             ⑤ ④ ③ ② ①
○ Select appropriate assessment methods and tools.                             ⑤ ④ ③ ② ①
○ Set data privacy and other ethical use policies.                             ⑤ ④ ③ ② ①
○ Create assessment plans.                                                     ⑤ ④ ③ ② ①
○ Develop, implement, and manage an assessment program.                        ⑤ ④ ③ ② ①
○ Schedule ongoing assessment activities based on an agreed-upon assessment cycle.  ⑤ ④ ③ ② ①
○ Other: _____                      ⑤ ④ ③ ② ①
○ Other: _____                      ⑤ ④ ③ ② ①

**THINK**

How did this activity make me feel?

_____

_____

What questions do I have?

_____

_____

What do I want to learn more about?

_____

_____

What innovative ideas have emerged?

_____

_____

**TALK**

What does this mean for my library? For me, as a librarian?

_____

_____

What do we need to do differently, as a library?

_____

_____

What does this make me want to continue to do, do better, or do differently, as a librarian?

_____

_____

**TARGET**

| Action | Timeframe | Responsible Parties | Follow-Up |
|---|---|---|---|
| **Options to Consider**<br>• Contact colleague<br>• Make decision<br>• Take action<br>• Ask question<br>• Get evidence/data | **When to Do It**<br>• Today<br>• This week<br>• This month<br>• This semester<br>• This year<br>• 2-3 year plan | **Who to Involve**<br>• Students<br>• Staff<br>• Librarians<br>• Administrators<br>• Faculty | **What to Do Next**<br>After I complete this action, what's the next step? |
|  |  |  |  |
|  |  |  |  |
|  |  |  |  |
|  |  |  |  |
|  |  |  |  |

# PROFESSIONAL DEVELOPMENT PLAN

**GETTING ORGANIZED**

## Goal
Develop a personal or library-wide professional development plan.

## Why
To fully engage in library value, impact, and assessment processes, librarians need to seek out professional development opportunities.

## Directions
1. Select professional development opportunities to pursue from the list provided; add any that are missing.
2. Estimate a timeframe for pursuing each professional development opportunity.
3. Determine the steps you will take to prepare for each professional development opportunity.
4. Engage the **T3** process.

## Suggested Reading
Oakleaf, Megan. *The Value of Academic Libraries: A Comprehensive Research Review and Report*. Chicago: ACRL, 2010. 99–100.

## See Also
Activity #19: Skill Audit

## Professional Development Opportunities

○ Inventory existing assessment skills.

○ Develop assessment reading lists, professional shelves, or online resources.

○ Form a library assessment committee.

○ Schedule consultant visits.

○ Take advantage of campus learning opportunities.

○ Attend library assessment webinars and conferences.

○ Attend higher education assessment conferences.

○ Engage The Value of Academic Libraries research agenda.

○ Present and publish in-progress or completed assessment projects.

○ Other: _____

_____

_____

_____

_____

○ Other: _____

_____

_____

_____

_____

○ Other: _____

_____

_____

_____

_____

| Professional Development Opportunity | Timeframe | Steps to Prepare |
|---|---|---|
| | ○ Today<br>○ This Week<br>○ This Month<br>○ This Semester<br>○ This Year<br>○ 2-3 Year Plan | 1.<br>2.<br>3.<br>4.<br>5. |
| | ○ Today<br>○ This Week<br>○ This Month<br>○ This Semester<br>○ This Year<br>○ 2-3 Year Plan | 1.<br>2.<br>3.<br>4.<br>5. |
| | ○ Today<br>○ This Week<br>○ This Month<br>○ This Semester<br>○ This Year<br>○ 2-3 Year Plan | 1.<br>2.<br>3.<br>4.<br>5. |
| | ○ Today<br>○ This Week<br>○ This Month<br>○ This Semester<br>○ This Year<br>○ 2-3 Year Plan | 1.<br>2.<br>3.<br>4.<br>5. |
| | ○ Today<br>○ This Week<br>○ This Month<br>○ This Semester<br>○ This Year<br>○ 2-3 Year Plan | 1.<br>2.<br>3.<br>4.<br>5. |

**THINK**

How did this activity make me feel?

_____

_____

What questions do I have?

_____

_____

What do I want to learn more about?

_____

_____

What innovative ideas have emerged?

_____

_____

**TALK**

What does this mean for my library? For me, as a librarian?

_____

_____

What do we need to do differently, as a library?

_____

_____

What does this make me want to continue to do, do better, or do differently, as a librarian?

_____

_____

**TARGET**

| Action | Timeframe | Responsible Parties | Follow-Up |
|---|---|---|---|
| **Options to Consider** <br> • Contact colleague <br> • Make decision <br> • Take action <br> • Ask question <br> • Get evidence/data | **When to Do It** <br> • Today <br> • This week <br> • This month <br> • This semester <br> • This year <br> • 2-3 year plan | **Who to Involve** <br> • Students <br> • Staff <br> • Librarians <br> • Administrators <br> • Faculty | **What to Do Next** <br> After I complete this action, what's the next step? |
|  |  |  |  |
|  |  |  |  |
|  |  |  |  |
|  |  |  |  |
|  |  |  |  |

# PLANNING FOR ORGANIZATIONAL CHANGE

**RE-THINKING**

### Goal

Gather ideas for changes brainstormed in the "What do we need to do differently, as a library?" prompts of the T3 sections of each activity.

### Why

To change practice, librarians need to integrate transformed thinking systematically throughout the library organization; categorizing ideas for change is a crucial first step in planning their implementation.

### Directions

1. At the close of each activity, capture the changes in each T3 section that could/should take place in the library.
2. Enter these changes in the appropriate "bucket."
3. When a number of changes have been amassed, engage the **T3** process again.

> " It is difficult to imagine how a department, division, or whole campus would reorient thought and action to address its accountability . . . without questioning existing organizational structures, the current allocation of resources, and established goals and priorities."
>
> **—RICHARD KEELING**

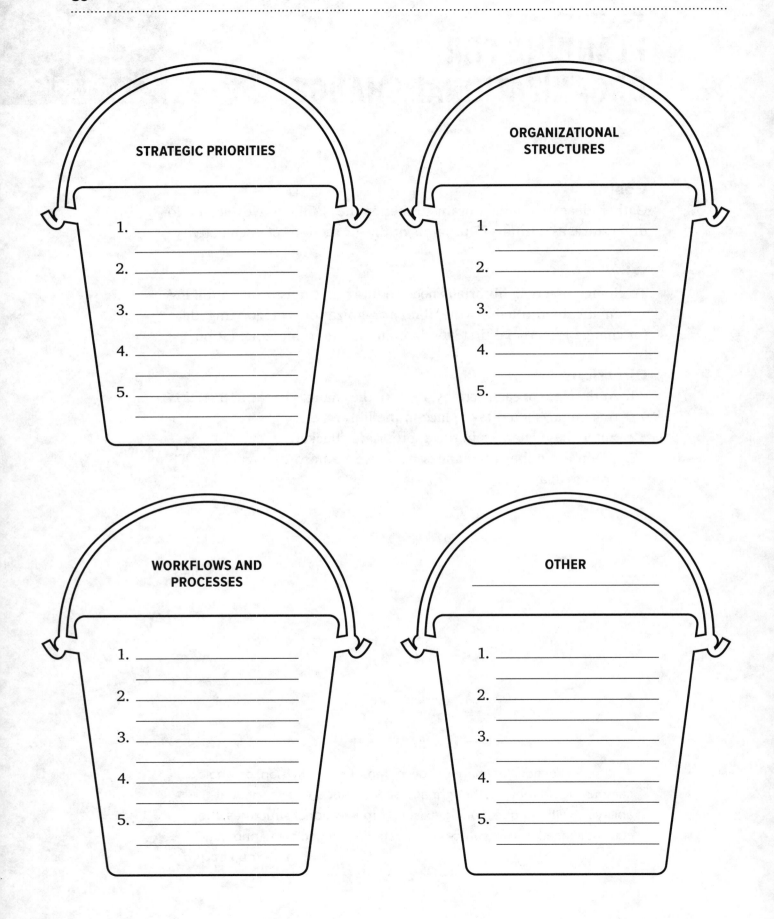

**STRATEGIC PRIORITIES**

1. _____
   _____
2. _____
   _____
3. _____
   _____
4. _____
   _____
5. _____
   _____

**ORGANIZATIONAL STRUCTURES**

1. _____
   _____
2. _____
   _____
3. _____
   _____
4. _____
   _____
5. _____
   _____

**WORKFLOWS AND PROCESSES**

1. _____
   _____
2. _____
   _____
3. _____
   _____
4. _____
   _____
5. _____
   _____

**OTHER**
_____

1. _____
   _____
2. _____
   _____
3. _____
   _____
4. _____
   _____
5. _____
   _____

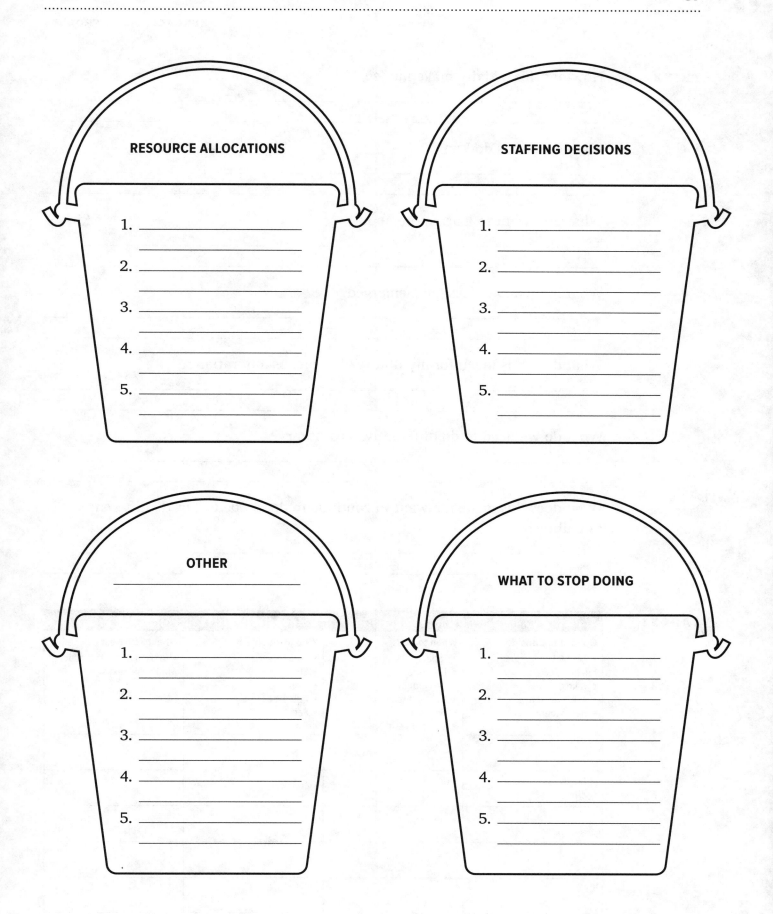

**RESOURCE ALLOCATIONS**

1. _____
   _____
2. _____
   _____
3. _____
   _____
4. _____
   _____
5. _____
   _____

**STAFFING DECISIONS**

1. _____
   _____
2. _____
   _____
3. _____
   _____
4. _____
   _____
5. _____
   _____

**OTHER**
_____

1. _____
   _____
2. _____
   _____
3. _____
   _____
4. _____
   _____
5. _____
   _____

**WHAT TO STOP DOING**

1. _____
   _____
2. _____
   _____
3. _____
   _____
4. _____
   _____
5. _____
   _____

**THINK**   How did this activity make me feel?

_____

_____

What questions do I have?

_____

_____

What do I want to learn more about?

_____

_____

What innovative ideas have emerged?

_____

_____

**TALK**   What does this mean for my library? For me, as a librarian?

_____

_____

What do we need to do differently, as a library?

_____

_____

What does this make me want to continue to do, do better, or do differently, as a librarian?

_____

_____

**TARGET**

| Action | Timeframe | Responsible Parties | Follow-Up |
|---|---|---|---|
| **Options to Consider**<br>• Contact colleague<br>• Make decision<br>• Take action<br>• Ask question<br>• Get evidence/data | **When to Do It**<br>• Today<br>• This week<br>• This month<br>• This semester<br>• This year<br>• 2-3 year plan | **Who to Involve**<br>• Students<br>• Staff<br>• Librarians<br>• Administrators<br>• Faculty | **What to Do Next**<br>After I complete this action, what's the next step? |
|  |  |  |  |
|  |  |  |  |
|  |  |  |  |
|  |  |  |  |
|  |  |  |  |

**ACTIVITY #22**

# PLANNING TIMELINE FOR CHANGE

**GETTING ORGANIZED**

### Goal

Gather ideas for changes brainstormed in the "Timeframe" prompts of the T3 sections of each activity.

### Why

To change practice, librarians need to set timelines for implementing plans to develop and demonstrate library contributions to institutional focus areas.

### Directions

1. At the close of each activity, capture the actions and timeframes generated in each T3 section.
2. Enter these actions in the appropriate timeframe.
3. When a number of actions have been amassed, engage the **T3** process again.

### Actions to Take Today

_____

_____

_____

_____

_____

_____

### Actions to Take This Week

_____

_____

_____

_____

_____

_____

### Actions to Take This Month

_____

_____

_____

_____

_____

_____

## Actions to Take This Semester

_____

_____

_____

_____

_____

_____

_____

## Actions to Take This Year

_____

_____

_____

_____

_____

_____

_____

## Actions to Take Over the Next 2–3 Years

_____

_____

_____

_____

_____

_____

_____

**THINK**         How did this activity make me feel?

_____

_____

What questions do I have?

_____

_____

What do I want to learn more about?

_____

_____

What innovative ideas have emerged?

_____

_____

**TALK**         What does this mean for my library? For me, as a librarian?

_____

_____

What do we need to do differently, as a library?

_____

_____

What does this make me want to continue to do, do better, or do differently, as a librarian?

_____

_____

**TARGET**

| Action | Timeframe | Responsible Parties | Follow-Up |
|---|---|---|---|
| **Options to Consider** <br> • Contact colleague <br> • Make decision <br> • Take action <br> • Ask question <br> • Get evidence/data | **When to Do It** <br> • Today <br> • This week <br> • This month <br> • This semester <br> • This year <br> • 2-3 year plan | **Who to Involve** <br> • Students <br> • Staff <br> • Librarians <br> • Administrators <br> • Faculty | **What to Do Next** <br> After I complete this action, what's the next step? |
|  |  |  |  |
|  |  |  |  |
|  |  |  |  |
|  |  |  |  |
|  |  |  |  |

ACTIVITY #23

# ASSESSMENT QUESTIONS FOR PROSPECTIVE LIBRARY HIRES

**TAKING ACTION**

## Goal

Investigate assessment knowledge, skills, and abilities of prospective library hires.

## Why

In order to build assessment capacity within a library organization, librarians need to identify prospective hires with assessment knowledge, skills, and abilities.

## Directions

1. Consider the list of interview questions; add any that are missing.
2. Check off questions to use in an interview.
3. Optional: Find a partner and assign roles: interviewee and interviewer. Role-play, then analyze your dialogue to determine what makes a good or poor response.
4. Engage the **T3** process.

## Suggested Readings

Oakleaf, Megan. "Are They Learning? Are We? Learning and the Academic Library." *Library Quarterly*. 81(1). 2011. 61–82.

Oakleaf, Megan and Scott Walter. "Recruitment for Results: Assessment Skills and the Academic Job Market." *Proceedings of the Library Assessment Conference*. Baltimore, MD: Association of Research Libraries. 2010.

## Higher Education and Institutional Contexts

What do you think are the most important issues facing higher education today?

_____

_____

Which multi-institutional assessment initiatives do you believe hold the most promise for meaningful comparisons of higher education institutions?

_____

_____

What role do you think the library should have in institutional program review and accreditation processes?

_____

_____

What do you think are the most important institutional focus areas on our campus?

_____

_____

These are the three most important institutional focus areas at our institution: [list]. How do you think the library can or does contribute to them?

_____

_____

Assuming some stakeholders do not realize the library's contribution to institutional focus areas, how would you go about increasing the visibility of these contributions?

_____

_____

Of course, the library is not the only contributor to these institutional focus areas. What strategies do you think you would use to stay abreast of assessment activities across our institution?

_____

_____

_____

How would you determine who the library should partner with to increase our contributions to institutional focus areas?  How would you approach these partners? How would you develop and manage these partnerships over time?

_____

_____

Other: _____

Other: _____

## Assessment Skills

What experience do you have in assessing library contributions to institutional focus areas?

_____

_____

Describe your process for defining and refining library outcomes in the context of institutional focus areas?

_____

_____

If you were tasked with creating an assessment plan for the library, what components would you include? What process would you follow?

_____

_____

What strategies do you use to select assessment methods or tools for a particular assessment project? Which methods or tools do you feel most comfortable with?

_____

_____

Do you have any assessment skills that you could envision sharing with other librarians?

_____

_____

Other: _____

Other: _____

## Assessment Data

How do you determine when assessment data is needed?

_____

_____

_____

Imagine you were responsible for analyzing and interpreting assessment data. What would you do? What challenges would you anticipate?

_____

_____

_____

What data analysis, visualization, management, or reporting systems are you familiar with?

_____

_____

_____

Tell us about a time you had to report or communicate data to a stakeholder. What went well? What did you learn? What do you wish you had done differently?

_____

_____

_____

What are your personal "best practices" for using data to make decisions and take actions?

_____

_____

_____

Other: _____

Other: _____

**ENGAGE THE T3 PROCESS**

How did this activity make me feel?                                                    **THINK**

_____

_____

What questions do I have?

_____

_____

What do I want to learn more about?

_____

_____

What innovative ideas have emerged?

_____

_____

What does this mean for my library? For me, as a librarian?                            **TALK**

_____

_____

What do we need to do differently, as a library?

_____

_____

What does this make me want to continue to do, do better, or do differently,
as a librarian?

_____

_____

| Action | Timeframe | Responsible Parties | Follow-Up | **TARGET** |
|---|---|---|---|---|
| **Options to Consider**<br>• Contact colleague<br>• Make decision<br>• Take action<br>• Ask question<br>• Get evidence/data | **When to Do It**<br>• Today<br>• This week<br>• This month<br>• This semester<br>• This year<br>• 2-3 year plan | **Who to Involve**<br>• Students<br>• Staff<br>• Librarians<br>• Administrators<br>• Faculty | **What to Do Next**<br>After I complete this action, what's the next step? | |
| | | | | |
| | | | | |
| | | | | |
| | | | | |
| | | | | |

# TO ASSESS OR NOT TO ASSESS

**LISTENING**

### Goal
Balance "concerns about" with "purposes for" assessment.

### Why
To motivate others to engage in assessment, librarians need to consider common librarian concerns about assessment.

### Directions
1. Find a partner.
2. Assign roles: librarian with assessment concerns and librarian advocating assessment.
3. Librarian with assessment concerns: Select a reason not to engage in assessment. Consider the reasons supplied; add ones that are missing.
4. Librarian advocating assessment: Select a reason to engage in assessment. Consider the reasons supplied; add ones that are missing.
5. Role-play a conversation discussing concerns about and purposes for assessment.
6. Choose new roles or reasons and repeat.
7. Engage the **T3** process.

# Reasons NOT to Engage in Assessment

Assessment is just a buzz-word. It too shall pass.

We don't have the skills/expertise to do assessment.

We don't have time to do assessment. Besides, I have to spend my time doing [non-assessment job task].

What if we find out we're not contributing to [institutional focus area]? That will look terrible and be used against us.

I'm not sure we're even supposed to do assessment. No one has told us to, and I don't think anyone expects us to.

There is no one to help us do assessment.

We don't make decisions or changes based on data and evidence anyway, so why bother?

Isn't assessment a faculty responsibility?

We already do a bunch of surveys and collect a ton of data. Why do more?

We can't isolate the library's contribution to [institutional focus area], so why bother?

We can't get access to the data we need to show library impact on individuals. Besides, using data on individuals is unethical.

No one will collaborate with me.

## Reasons to Engage in Assessment

Knowledge is power, right? We need to know if we're making an impact so we can celebrate our successes and address our weaknesses.

Maybe we'll find out there's something we can stop doing!

Without data, we can't argue for resources that will provide us with more money, staff, or time.

Assessment is a professional ethic. We should be guided by concepts of reflective practice and continuous improvement—both are supported by assessment.

It would be better to find out about any problems now, rather than to go on committing errors in perpetuity.

We have evidence and data, we can make decisions based on that, not "educated guesses" and hope.

We can engage in professional development to close any assessment skill gaps.

If we keep waiting for other people to ask us to provide assessment data, we are being passive, not active. We need to come to the table and bring our own chair.

All endeavors benefit from constructive criticism, and your concerns about assessment could help us make sure our assessment efforts are as good as possible.

The most meaningful evidence is often challenging to gather, but it pays off the most too. If we put effort in on the front end, we'll be happy we did when we get data we can actually use to make decisions. There's no point in collecting "easy," but ultimately meaningless, data.

Not having the right data is not an excuse for not collecting it.

All higher education professionals should reflect on their efforts and strive for improvement. If others don't expect us to assess, they should!

No one in higher education can say that they—and only they—make a causal difference. No one acts alone, nor need they. The point is to reach a great outcome as an institution.

Through campus partnerships, we can get access to the data and expertise we need to do assessment in the library.

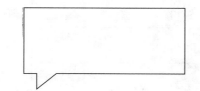

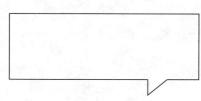

**THINK**

How did this activity make me feel?

_____

_____

What questions do I have?

_____

_____

What do I want to learn more about?

_____

_____

What innovative ideas have emerged?

_____

_____

**TALK**

What does this mean for my library? For me, as a librarian?

_____

_____

What do we need to do differently, as a library?

_____

_____

What does this make me want to continue to do, do better, or do differently, as a librarian?

_____

_____

**TARGET**

| Action | Timeframe | Responsible Parties | Follow-Up |
|---|---|---|---|
| **Options to Consider**<br>• Contact colleague<br>• Make decision<br>• Take action<br>• Ask question<br>• Get evidence/data | **When to Do It**<br>• Today<br>• This week<br>• This month<br>• This semester<br>• This year<br>• 2-3 year plan | **Who to Involve**<br>• Students<br>• Staff<br>• Librarians<br>• Administrators<br>• Faculty | **What to Do Next**<br>After I complete this action, what's the next step? |
| | | | |
| | | | |
| | | | |
| | | | |
| | | | |

ACTIVITY #25

# ASSESSMENT FEARS, CHALLENGES, AND BARRIERS

**TAKING ACTION**

## Goal
Explore strategies to address common assessment fears, challenges, and barriers.

## Why
To prepare for challenges frequently encountered when seeking to demonstrate library contributions to institutional focus areas, librarians need to brainstorm and proactively engage strategies for overcoming them.

## Directions
1. Consider the list of common challenges of demonstrating the contributions of library services, expertise, and resources to institutional focus areas; add any that are missing.
2. Check off the challenges you expect to encounter.
3. Select two challenges; enter them at the top of each column.
4. Respond to the Reflection Questions for each challenge; consider the strategies listed.
5. Engage the **T3** process.

## Suggested Readings
Oakleaf, Megan and Lisa Hinchliffe. "Assessment Cycle or Circular File: Do Academic Librarians Use Information Literacy Assessment Data?" *Proceedings of the Library Assessment Conference.* Seattle, WA: Association of Research Libraries. 2008.

Eldredge, Jonathan. "Cognitive Biases as Obstacles to Effective Decision Making in EBLIP." *4th International Evidence Based Library and Information Practice Conference.* Durham, NC: 2007.

## What is the Challenge?

○ Too little time
○ Too few financial resources
○ Too few staff resources
○ Too few rewards
○ Lack of knowledge or skills
○ Lack of support structures
   (e.g., point person, committee)

○ Lack of collaborators/partners
○ Lack of clear expectations/role
○ Lack of interest
○ Lack of trust or toleration
   for risk-taking
○ Lack of tools/techniques

○ Other: _____

○ Other: _____

## What Strategies Can You Use?

### Challenge #1 _____

**Reflection Questions**

1. Describe and analyze the challenge in detail. What are the component parts of this challenge?

   _____

   _____

2. What general strategies can you use to meet or mitigate this challenge?

   _____

   _____

3. What educational or professional development strategies might you employ?

   _____

   _____

4. What collaborations or partnerships might be useful?

   _____

   _____

5. What reallocations or prioritizations might be necessary?

   _____

   _____

6. How can you "get started" despite remaining challenges?

   _____

   _____

## What are the Strategies?

○ Educate

○ Collaborate

○ Coordinate

○ Celebrate

○ Clarify

○ Reallocate

○ Prioritize

○ Be flexible

○ Start small

**Challenge #2** _____

**Reflection Questions**

1. Describe and analyze the challenge in detail. What are the component parts of this challenge?

   _____

   _____

2. What general strategies can you use to meet or mitigate this challenge?

   _____

   _____

3. What educational or professional development strategies might you employ?

   _____

   _____

4. What collaborations or partnerships might be useful?

   _____

   _____

5. What reallocations or prioritizations might be necessary?

   _____

   _____

6. How can you "get started" despite remaining challenges?

   _____

   _____

**THINK**

How did this activity make me feel?

_____

_____

What questions do I have?

_____

_____

What do I want to learn more about?

_____

_____

What innovative ideas have emerged?

_____

_____

**TALK**

What does this mean for my library? For me, as a librarian?

_____

_____

What do we need to do differently, as a library?

_____

_____

What does this make me want to continue to do, do better, or do differently, as a librarian?

_____

_____

**TARGET**

| Action | Timeframe | Responsible Parties | Follow-Up |
|---|---|---|---|
| **Options to Consider**<br>• Contact colleague<br>• Make decision<br>• Take action<br>• Ask question<br>• Get evidence/data | **When to Do It**<br>• Today<br>• This week<br>• This month<br>• This semester<br>• This year<br>• 2-3 year plan | **Who to Involve**<br>• Students<br>• Staff<br>• Librarians<br>• Administrators<br>• Faculty | **What to Do Next**<br>After I complete this action, what's the next step? |
| | | | |
| | | | |
| | | | |
| | | | |
| | | | |

# LIBRARY IMPACT MAP

## Goal
Align library services, expertise, and resources with institutional focus areas.

## Why
To link library contributions and institutional focus areas, librarians need to identify the services, expertise, and resources that impact or contribute to each institutional focus area.

## Directions
1. Consider the left column. Are all your institutional focus areas listed? Cross out focus areas that do not apply; add any that are missing.
2. Consider the top row. Are all your library's key services, expertise, and resources listed? Cross out services, expertise, or resources that do not apply; add any that are missing.
3. Work through the map one row or column at a time. In each intersecting cell, enter:
   - **Y** = Yes, we believe there is an impact relationship between this institutional focus area and this library service, expertise, or resource.
   - **Y+** = Yes, there is an impact, and we have evidence/data of the impact.
   - **Y++** = Yes, there is impact, we have evidence/data, and we've communicated the impact to stakeholders.
   - **CB** = There "could be" an impact if we did something better or differently.
   - **N** = No, there is no impact.
4. Engage the **T3** process.

## Suggested Reading
Oakleaf, Megan. "Are They Learning? Are We? Learning and the Academic Library." *Library Quarterly*. 81(1). 2011. 61–82.

## See Also
Activity #1: Institutional Focus Areas

# Library Services, Expertise, and Resources

| INSTITUTIONAL FOCUS AREAS | Reference, Physical | Reference, Digital | Reference, Subject Guides | Reference, Roving | Reference, Embedded | Reference, Consultations | Outreach | Liaison Services | Embedded/Mobile Services | Instruction, One-Shot | Instruction, Course-Integrated | Instruction, Curriculum-Integrated | Instruction, Credit Course | Instruction, Embedded | Instruction, Drop-In | Collection Development | Collections, General | Collections, Special Topics |
|---|---|---|---|---|---|---|---|---|---|---|---|---|---|---|---|---|---|---|
| Student Recruitment, Enrollment | | | | | | | | | | | | | | | | | | |
| Student Retention, Completion, Graduation | | | | | | | | | | | | | | | | | | |
| Student Career Success | | | | | | | | | | | | | | | | | | |
| Student GPA, Test Achievement | | | | | | | | | | | | | | | | | | |
| Student Learning Outcomes | | | | | | | | | | | | | | | | | | |
| Student Experience, Engagement | | | | | | | | | | | | | | | | | | |
| Student-Faculty Academic Rapport | | | | | | | | | | | | | | | | | | |
| Alumni Lifelong Learning | | | | | | | | | | | | | | | | | | |
| Faculty Recruitment, Tenure, Promotion | | | | | | | | | | | | | | | | | | |
| Faculty Teaching | | | | | | | | | | | | | | | | | | |
| Faculty Service | | | | | | | | | | | | | | | | | | |
| Faculty Research Productivity | | | | | | | | | | | | | | | | | | |
| Faculty Grant Seeking | | | | | | | | | | | | | | | | | | |
| Faculty Patents, Technology Transfer | | | | | | | | | | | | | | | | | | |
| Faculty Innovation, Entrepreneurship | | | | | | | | | | | | | | | | | | |
| Institutional Prestige | | | | | | | | | | | | | | | | | | |
| Institutional Affordability | | | | | | | | | | | | | | | | | | |
| Institutional Efficiencies | | | | | | | | | | | | | | | | | | |
| Institutional Accreditation, Program Review | | | | | | | | | | | | | | | | | | |
| Institutional Brand | | | | | | | | | | | | | | | | | | |
| Institutional Athletics | | | | | | | | | | | | | | | | | | |
| Institutional Development, Funding, Endowments | | | | | | | | | | | | | | | | | | |
| Local, Global Workforce Development | | | | | | | | | | | | | | | | | | |
| Local, Global Economic Growth | | | | | | | | | | | | | | | | | | |
| Local, Global Engagement, Community-Building, Social Inclusion | | | | | | | | | | | | | | | | | | |
| Other: | | | | | | | | | | | | | | | | | | |
| Other: | | | | | | | | | | | | | | | | | | |
| Other: | | | | | | | | | | | | | | | | | | |
| Other: | | | | | | | | | | | | | | | | | | |
| Other: | | | | | | | | | | | | | | | | | | |

**Y** = Yes, we believe there is an impact relationship between this institutional focus area and this library service, expertise, or resource. **Y +** = Yes, there is an impact, and we have evidence/data of the impact. **Y + +** = Yes, there is impact, we have evidence/data, and we've communicated the impact to stakeholders. **CB** = There "could be" an impact if we did something better or differently. **N** = No, there is no impact.

| Collections, Reference | Collections, Popular | Collections, Government Documents | Collections, Data/Statistics | Collections, E-Resources | Collections, E-Books | Collections, Multimedia | Collections, Technology | Special Collections | Archives | Institutional Repositories | Data Repositories | Circulation | Acquisitions | Cataloging | Interlibrary Loan | Reserves | Copyright Services | Disability Services | Library Systems | Library Website | Library Social Media | Library Communications | Friends of the Library | Facilities, General | Facilities, Study Space | Facilities, Computing Space | Facilities, Carrels | Facilities, Learning Commons | Other: | Other: | Other: | Other: |
|---|---|---|---|---|---|---|---|---|---|---|---|---|---|---|---|---|---|---|---|---|---|---|---|---|---|---|---|---|---|---|---|---|
| | | | | | | | | | | | | | | | | | | | | | | | | | | | | | | | | |

**THINK**

How did this activity make me feel?

_____

_____

What questions do I have?

_____

_____

What do I want to learn more about?

_____

_____

What innovative ideas have emerged?

_____

**TALK**

What does this mean for my library? For me, as a librarian?

_____

_____

What do we need to do differently, as a library?

_____

_____

What does this make me want to continue to do, do better, or do differently, as a librarian?

_____

_____

**TARGET**

| Action | Timeframe | Responsible Parties | Follow-Up |
|---|---|---|---|
| **Options to Consider**<br>• Contact colleague<br>• Make decision<br>• Take action<br>• Ask question<br>• Get evidence/data | **When to Do It**<br>• Today<br>• This week<br>• This month<br>• This semester<br>• This year<br>• 2-3 year plan | **Who to Involve**<br>• Students<br>• Staff<br>• Librarians<br>• Administrators<br>• Faculty | **What to Do Next**<br>After I complete this action, what's the next step? |
| | | | |
| | | | |
| | | | |
| | | | |
| | | | |

# PRESENT AND FUTURE LIBRARY IMPACT

**RE-THINKING**

## Goal

Link present and future library contributions to institutional focus areas.

## Why

To analyze and expand library contributions to institutional focus areas, librarians need to identify existing as well as potential library services, expertise, and resources.

## Directions

1. Consider the left column. Are all your institutional focus areas listed? Cross out focus areas that do not apply; add any that are missing.
2. Consider the current and possible library contributions to institutional focus areas.
3. List the ways in which the library currently contributes to each institutional focus area.
4. Brainstorm ways in which the library could contribute to each institutional focus area if it did something differently or better.
5. Engage the **T3** process.

## See Also

Activity #1: Institutional Focus Areas
Activity #2: Stakeholders as the Heart of the Institution
Activity #26: Library Impact Map

| INSTITUTIONAL FOCUS | What contributions *does* the library make?<br>"We enable [stakeholder] to achieve [goal/task/outcome]." |
|---|---|
| Student Recruitment, Enrollment | |
| Student Retention, Completion, Graduation | |
| Student Career Success | |
| Student GPA, Test Achievement | |
| Student Learning Outcomes | |
| Student Experience, Engagement | |
| Student-Faculty Academic Rapport | |
| Alumni Lifelong Learning | |
| Faculty Recruitment, Tenure, Promotion | |
| Faculty Teaching | |
| Faculty Service | |
| Faculty Research Productivity | |
| Faculty Grant Seeking | |
| Faculty Patents, Technology Transfer | |
| Faculty Innovation, Entrepreneurship | |
| Institutional Prestige | |
| Institutional Affordability | |
| Institutional Efficiencies | |
| Institutional Accreditation, Program Review | |
| Institutional Brand | |
| Institutional Athletics | |
| Institutional Development, Funding, Endowments | |
| Local, Global Workforce Development | |
| Local, Global Economic Growth | |
| Local, Global Engagement, Community-Building, Social Inclusion | |
| Other: | |
| Other: | |
| Other: | |
| Other: | |
| Other: | |

**What contributions *could* the library make?**
"If we did something differently or better, we could enable [stakeholder] to achieve [goal/task/outcome]."

**THINK**

How did this activity make me feel?

_____
_____

What questions do I have?

_____
_____

What do I want to learn more about?

_____
_____

What innovative ideas have emerged?

_____
_____

**TALK**

What does this mean for my library? For me, as a librarian?

_____
_____

What do we need to do differently, as a library?

_____
_____

What does this make me want to continue to do, do better, or do differently, as a librarian?

_____
_____

**TARGET**

| Action | Timeframe | Responsible Parties | Follow-Up |
|---|---|---|---|
| **Options to Consider**<br>• Contact colleague<br>• Make decision<br>• Take action<br>• Ask question<br>• Get evidence/data | **When to Do It**<br>• Today<br>• This week<br>• This month<br>• This semester<br>• This year<br>• 2-3 year plan | **Who to Involve**<br>• Students<br>• Staff<br>• Librarians<br>• Administrators<br>• Faculty | **What to Do Next**<br>After I complete this action, what's the next step? |
|  |  |  |  |
|  |  |  |  |
|  |  |  |  |
|  |  |  |  |
|  |  |  |  |

# PASSIVE-TO-ACTIVE IMPACT

## Goal

Transform passive library services, expertise, and resources into active creation of stakeholder library interactions.

## Why

To maximize library contributions to institutional focus areas, librarians need to recreate existing services, expertise, and resources into more active engagements with stakeholders.

## Directions

1. Enter existing, passive library services, expertise, and resources in the left column.
2. Brainstorm revised, active versions of the same services, expertise, or resources in the middle column. Optional: State the institutional focus area this revised library service, expertise, or resource impacts.
3. Determine whether the brainstormed active library service, expertise, or resource is worth pursuing; indicate the decision in the right column.
4. Engage the **T3** process.

| PASSIVE | ACTIVE | DECISION |
|---|---|---|
| Librarians answer reference questions. | Librarians answer reference questions with intent to instruct (student learning outcomes) or establish academic rapport (student experience, engagement). | ○ Pursue<br>○ Pursue at a later date<br>○ Do not pursue |
| Library resources provide content for faculty publications and grants. | Librarians provide executive summaries, prepare annotated bibliographies, or help author literature reviews for faculty publications (faculty research productivity) and grant proposals (faculty grant seeking). | ○ Pursue<br>○ Pursue at a later date<br>○ Do not pursue |
| Library resources include faculty publications. | Librarians track citations and prepare "who's citing you" reports for faculty (faculty tenure, promotion). Librarians "push" impact factor and acceptance rates to faculty applying for tenure/promotion (faculty recruitment). | ○ Pursue<br>○ Pursue at a later date<br>○ Do not pursue |
| Library resources, especially business databases, include company information and profiles. | Librarians provide company information and profiles to students interviewing for jobs and internships (student career success). | ○ Pursue<br>○ Pursue at a later date<br>○ Do not pursue |
| Librarians create online instructional materials for students. | Librarians teach parents information literacy skills at new student orientation, workshops for parents, parents' weekend programming, or "pushed" online methods (student learning outcomes). | ○ Pursue<br>○ Pursue at a later date<br>○ Do not pursue |
| Librarians prepare "honorary degree" candidate materials for senior institutional administration/leaders upon request. | Librarians market and provide executive summaries on topics related to institutional decision-making to senior institutional administration/leaders or their assistants (institutional efficiencies). | ○ Pursue<br>○ Pursue at a later date<br>○ Do not pursue |
| Library provides a "library fact sheet" or brochure for faculty candidates. | Librarians schedule time on interview schedules to discuss alert services, collection resources, etc., in areas of faculty candidates' research and teaching interests (faculty recruitment). | ○ Pursue<br>○ Pursue at a later date<br>○ Do not pursue |
|  |  | ○ Pursue<br>○ Pursue at a later date<br>○ Do not pursue |
|  |  | ○ Pursue<br>○ Pursue at a later date<br>○ Do not pursue |
|  |  | ○ Pursue<br>○ Pursue at a later date<br>○ Do not pursue |
|  |  | ○ Pursue<br>○ Pursue at a later date<br>○ Do not pursue |

**ENGAGE THE T3 PROCESS**

How did this activity make me feel?                                              THINK

_____
_____

What questions do I have?

_____
_____

What do I want to learn more about?

_____
_____

What innovative ideas have emerged?

_____
_____

What does this mean for my library? For me, as a librarian?                     TALK

_____
_____

What do we need to do differently, as a library?

_____
_____

What does this make me want to continue to do, do better, or do differently,
as a librarian?

_____
_____

TARGET

| Action | Timeframe | Responsible Parties | Follow-Up |
|---|---|---|---|
| **Options to Consider**<br>• Contact colleague<br>• Make decision<br>• Take action<br>• Ask question<br>• Get evidence/data | **When to Do It**<br>• Today<br>• This week<br>• This month<br>• This semester<br>• This year<br>• 2-3 year plan | **Who to Involve**<br>• Students<br>• Staff<br>• Librarians<br>• Administrators<br>• Faculty | **What to Do Next**<br>After I complete this action, what's the next step? |
|  |  |  |  |
|  |  |  |  |
|  |  |  |  |
|  |  |  |  |
|  |  |  |  |

# IMPACT VISION CREATION

## Goal

Depict the library's current contribution to institutional focus areas and envision its future contributions.

## Why

To enact changes to the library's contribution to institutional focus areas, librarians need to envision what those changes "look like."

## Directions

1. Consider how the library looks from a stakeholder perspective. If a stakeholder peered through a library window, what would s/he see?
2. Draw the current state of the library from a stakeholder perspective.
3. Respond to Reflection Questions #1–2.
4. Imagine how the library might look if it were more focused on contributing to institutional focus areas. Then what would a stakeholder looking through a window see?
5. Draw the future state of the library from a stakeholder perspective.
6. Respond to Reflection Questions #3–4.
7. Engage the **T3** process.

## How the Library Is . . .

## Reflection Questions

1. What are the most important components of your vision of the library as it currently exists?

   _____

   _____

2. What message do these components send about the current state of library contributions to institutional focus areas?

   _____

   _____

**. . . and How the Library Could Be**

3. What are the most important components of your vision of the library in the future?

   _____

   _____

4. What message do these components send about the future state of library contributions to institutional focus areas?

   _____

   _____

**THINK**

How did this activity make me feel?

_____

_____

What questions do I have?

_____

_____

What do I want to learn more about?

_____

_____

What innovative ideas have emerged?

_____

_____

**TALK**

What does this mean for my library? For me, as a librarian?

_____

_____

What do we need to do differently, as a library?

_____

_____

What does this make me want to continue to do, do better, or do differently, as a librarian?

_____

_____

**TARGET**

| Action | Timeframe | Responsible Parties | Follow-Up |
|---|---|---|---|
| **Options to Consider**<br>• Contact colleague<br>• Make decision<br>• Take action<br>• Ask question<br>• Get evidence/data | **When to Do It**<br>• Today<br>• This week<br>• This month<br>• This semester<br>• This year<br>• 2-3 year plan | **Who to Involve**<br>• Students<br>• Staff<br>• Librarians<br>• Administrators<br>• Faculty | **What to Do Next**<br>After I complete this action, what's the next step? |
| | | | |
| | | | |
| | | | |
| | | | |
| | | | |

ACTIVITY #30
# IMPACT ON STUDENT LEARNING OUTCOMES

**TAKING ACTION**

## Goal
Explore the existing and potential contribution of the library to student learning outcomes.

## Why
To analyze and expand the library's contribution to student learning outcomes, librarians need to articulate the library's impact in this institutional focus area, plan ways to assess that impact, anticipate possible assessment results, determine a reporting and communication strategy, and brainstorm future decisions and actions.

## Directions
1. Consider ways in which the library contributes to student learning outcomes.
2. Connect the dots, selecting an item(s) from each category (student library interaction, relationship type, learning outcome, learning assessment). Use them to draft a statement or question describing potential library contributions to student learning.

   *Examples:* "Student participation in reference transactions contributes to increased ability to locate information as demonstrated by student research logs." **OR** "Does student engagement in library instruction correlate with improved use of information as measured by student test scores?"

3. Brainstorm evidence/data sources that might exist for these items.
4. Suggest methods, tools, strategies, and techniques you might use to identify and analyze possible relationships between these items, as well as the resources you might need to support this effort.
5. List ideas for reporting or communicating the results of your analysis.
6. Anticipate decisions you could make or actions you could take based on your results.
7. Engage the **T3** process.

## Suggested Readings

Oakleaf, Megan. *The Value of Academic Libraries: A Comprehensive Research Review and Report.* Chicago: ACRL, 2010. 117–119.

Oakleaf, Megan. "Writing Information Literacy Assessment Plans: A Guide to Best Practice." *Communications in Information Literacy.* 3(2). 2010.

**123**

How do student **interactions** with the library                    **impact**

○ Library instruction engagement
○ Reference transactions
○ Resource usage (e.g., circulation, downloads, reserves)
○ "High library usage" course enrollment
○ "High library usage" cocurricular participation
○ Library facility usage
○ Other: _____
○ Other: _____
○ Other: _____
○ Other: _____

○ Contributive relationship
○ Correlative relationship
○ Causative relationship
○ Other: _____
○ Other: _____
○ Other: _____
○ Other: _____

### CONNECT THE DOTS

1. Connect the dots, selecting an item(s) from each box above. Use the selected items to compose a statement or question describing potential library contributions to student learning.

   _____

   _____

2. What evidence/data sources exist for each item in your statement/question?

   _____

   _____

3. How might you identify and analyze possible relationships among these items?

   _____

   _____

4. What other factors do you need to control when investigating possible relationships?

   _____

   _____

student learning **outcomes** as demonstrated by learning **assessments?**

▼                                        ▼

- ○ Define information needs
- ○ Locate information
- ○ Evaluate information
- ○ Use information
- ○ Use information ethically and responsibly
- ○ "Authority Is Constructed and Contextual" outcomes
- ○ "Information Creation as a Process" outcomes
- ○ "Information Has Value" outcomes
- ○ "Research as Inquiry" outcomes
- ○ "Scholarship as Conversation" outcomes
- ○ "Searching as Strategic Exploration" outcomes
- ○ Other: _____
- ○ Other: _____
- ○ Other: _____
- ○ Other: _____

**Authentic, performance-based assessments (integrated into courses or cocurricular activities and assessed using rubrics or other scoring guides):**

- ○ Research logs
- ○ Research papers
- ○ Reflective writing
- ○ Open-ended question responses
- ○ Annotated bibliography
- ○ Worksheets
- ○ Concept maps
- ○ Tutorial responses
- ○ Group projects
- ○ Role plays
- ○ Performances
- ○ Speeches
- ○ Multimedia presentations
- ○ Lab reports
- ○ Posters
- ○ Exhibits
- ○ Portfolios
- ○ Other: _____
- ○ Other: _____

**Other assessments:**

- ○ Tests
- ○ Surveys
- ○ Assessment management system learning outcome evidence/data
- ○ Course grades and GPA
- ○ Other: _____
- ○ Other: _____

5. What resources do you need to support your effort?

_____

_____

_____

6. To whom will you report any relationships that emerge? How will those reports be structured, formatted, delivered, etc.?

_____

_____

_____

7. If a relationship is established, what decisions can you make? What actions can you take?

_____

_____

_____

**THINK**

How did this activity make me feel?

_____

_____

What questions do I have?

_____

_____

What do I want to learn more about?

_____

_____

What innovative ideas have emerged?

_____

_____

**TALK**

What does this mean for my library? For me, as a librarian?

_____

_____

What do we need to do differently, as a library?

_____

_____

What does this make me want to continue to do, do better, or do differently, as a librarian?

_____

_____

**TARGET**

| Action | | Timeframe | Responsible Parties | Follow-Up |
|---|---|---|---|---|
| **Options to Consider**<br>• Contact colleague<br>• Make decision<br>• Take action<br>• Ask question<br>• Get evidence/data | | **When to Do It**<br>• Today<br>• This week<br>• This month<br>• This semester<br>• This year<br>• 2-3 year plan | **Who to Involve**<br>• Students<br>• Staff<br>• Librarians<br>• Administrators<br>• Faculty | **What to Do Next**<br>After I complete this action, what's the next step? |
| | | | | |
| | | | | |
| | | | | |
| | | | | |
| | | | | |

# IMPACT ON STUDENT RETENTION

## Goal

Explore the existing and potential contributions of the library to student retention.

## Why

To analyze and expand the library's contribution to student retention, librarians need to identify existing and potential library services, expertise, and resources that impact this institutional focus area.

## Directions

1. Consider the institutional characteristics, high-impact practices, and student affairs programming linked to student retention; check off those that apply to your institution and add any that are missing.
2. Identify existing and potential library contributions to these characteristics, practices, and programs.
3. Respond to the Reflection Questions.
4. Engage the **T3** process.

## Suggested Readings

Oakleaf, Megan. *The Value of Academic Libraries: A Comprehensive Research Review and Report.* Chicago: ACRL, 2010. 32–35, 106–108.

Kuh, George D. *High-Impact Educational Practices.* Association of American Colleges and Universities, 2008.

> " Many students don't develop a connection with their institution. And when they don't, they leave."
>
> —JENNIFER GONZALEZ

# How *does/could* the library contribute to institutional charactistics, high-impact practices, and student affairs programming linked to retention?

| | Library does contribute | Library could contribute |
|---|---|---|
| **Institutional Characteristics** | | |
| ○ Social engagement and integration with peers | | |
| ○ Rapport with academic faculty, professionals, and staff | | |
| ○ Accessible academic support | | |
| ○ Accessible social support | | |
| ○ Expectations of success established by academic faculty, professionals, and staff | | |
| ○ Timely and descriptive feedback to students | | |
| ○ Other: | | |
| ○ Other: | | |
| **High-Impact Practices** | | |
| ○ First-year seminars and experiences | | |
| ○ Common intellectual experiences | | |
| ○ Learning communities | | |
| ○ Writing-intensive courses | | |
| ○ Collaborative assignments and projects | | |
| ○ Undergraduate research | | |
| ○ Diversity/global learning | | |
| ○ Service learning/community-based learning | | |
| ○ Internships | | |
| ○ Capstone courses and projects | | |
| ○ Other: | | |
| ○ Other: | | |
| **Student Affairs Programming** | | |
| ○ Admissions and new student orientation | | |
| ○ Residence life | | |
| ○ Greek life | | |
| ○ Study abroad | | |
| ○ Athletics and intramurals | | |
| ○ Other: | | |
| ○ Other: | | |

## Reflection Questions

1. What are the main ways your institution seeks to retain students?

   _____

   _____

   _____

2. What library services, expertise, or resources currently contribute to student retention efforts?

   _____

   _____

   _____

3. What current library services, expertise, or resources could contribute to student retention if they were refocused on academic rapport, integration, and enagement outcomes? If they were implemented differently or better?

   _____

   _____

   _____

4. What new library services, expertise, or resources could be designed and developed to contribute to student retention efforts?

   _____

   _____

   _____

5. What new library partnerships and collaborations could be developed and maintained to contribute to student retention efforts?

   _____

   _____

   _____

**THINK**

How did this activity make me feel?

_____

_____

What questions do I have?

_____

_____

What do I want to learn more about?

_____

_____

What innovative ideas have emerged?

_____

_____

**TALK**

What does this mean for my library? For me, as a librarian?

_____

_____

What do we need to do differently, as a library?

_____

_____

What does this make me want to continue to do, do better, or do differently, as a librarian?

_____

_____

**TARGET**

| Action | Timeframe | Responsible Parties | Follow-Up |
|---|---|---|---|
| **Options to Consider**<br>• Contact colleague<br>• Make decision<br>• Take action<br>• Ask question<br>• Get evidence/data | **When to Do It**<br>• Today<br>• This week<br>• This month<br>• This semester<br>• This year<br>• 2-3 year plan | **Who to Involve**<br>• Students<br>• Staff<br>• Librarians<br>• Administrators<br>• Faculty | **What to Do Next**<br>After I complete this action, what's the next step? |
| | | | |
| | | | |
| | | | |
| | | | |
| | | | |

## ACTIVITY #32
# IMPACT ON FACULTY PRODUCTIVITY

### Goal

Explore the existing and potential contributions of the library to faculty research and teaching productivity.

### Why

To analyze and expand library contributions to faculty, research and teaching, productivity, librarians need to articulate the library's impact on the institutional focus areas, plan ways to assess that impact, anticipate possible assessment results, determine a reporting and communication strategy, and brainstorm future decisions and actions.

### Directions

1. Consider ways in which the library contributes to faculty productivity.

2. In either the research or teaching area, connect the dots, selecting an item(s) from each category (faculty library interaction, relationship type, productivity measure). Use them to draft a statement or question describing potential library contributions to faculty productivity. *Examples*: "Faculty usage of library resources contributes to increased faculty publications." **OR** "Do librarian-faculty collaborations focused on cooperatively designed classroom assignments correlate with decreased time spent grading?"

3. Brainstorm evidence/data sources that might exist for these items.

4. Suggest methods, tools, strategies, and techniques you might use to identify and analyze possible relationships between these items, as well as the resources you might need to support this effort.

5. List ideas for reporting or communicating the results of your analysis.

6. Anticipate decisions you could make or actions you could take based on your results.

7. Engage the **T3** process.

### Suggested Reading

Oakleaf, Megan. *The Value of Academic Libraries: A Comprehensive Research Review and Report*. Chicago: ACRL, 2010. 46–49, 129–136.

## How do faculty **interactions** with the library

- ○ Librarian-faculty research collaborations to:
  - ○ Prepare publications
  - ○ Prepare presentations or exhibits
  - ○ Prepare grant proposals
  - ○ Prepare patent/technology transfer applications
  - ○ Prepare tenure and promotion packages
  - ○ Develop literature reviews and executive summaries
  - ○ Manage research projects
  - ○ Archive research outputs and data
  - ○ Develop library collections that support research
- ○ Reference transactions/consultations
- ○ Resource usage (e.g., circulation, downloads, reserve, alert profiles)
- ○ Resource interactions (e.g., reading, citing)
- ○ Library facility usage
- ○ Other: _____
- ○ Other: _____

## impact

- ○ Contributive relationship
- ○ Correlative relationship
- ○ Causative relationship
- ○ Other: _____
- ○ Other: _____

### CONNECT THE DOTS

## How do faculty **interactions** with the library

- ○ Librarian instructional support:
  - ○ Guest lectures
  - ○ Embedded online tutorials
  - ○ Subject guides
  - ○ Reserves/reading lists/textbooks
  - ○ Lecture content
- ○ Scholarship of teaching and learning collections
- ○ Librarian-faculty instructional collaborations:
  - ○ Develop assignments
  - ○ Develop courses
- ○ Develop curriculum
- ○ Other: _____
- ○ Other: _____

## impact

- ○ Contributive relationship
- ○ Correlative relationship
- ○ Causative relationship
- ○ Other: _____
- ○ Other: _____

### CONNECT THE DOTS

faculty **research** productivity?

▼

- ○ Increased publications
- ○ Increased presentations or exhibits
- ○ Increased grant proposals
- ○ Increased grants awarded
- ○ Increased patents or technology transfer
- ○ Increased awards
- ○ Increased citations
- ○ Increased impact measures (e.g., social media impact, journal impact factors, peer review)
- ○ Increased consultancy/advisory activity
- ○ Successful tenure and promotion cases
- ○ Other: _____
- ○ Other: _____

1. Connect the dots, selecting an item(s) from each box in either the research or teaching areas on the left. Compose a statement or question describing potential library contributions to faculty research productivity or faculty teaching productivity.

   _____
   _____

2. What evidence/data sources exist for each item in your statement/question?

   _____
   _____

3. How might you identify and analyze possible relationships among these items?

   _____
   _____

4. What other factors do you need to control when investigating possible relationships?

   _____
   _____

faculty **teaching** productivity?

▼

- ○ Faculty self-report:
  - ○ Improved faculty instructional skills
  - ○ Improved student learning experiences
  - ○ Increased scope of instructional resources
  - ○ Increased faculty research skills
  - ○ Instruction preparation time saved
  - ○ Student interaction time saved
  - ○ Grading time saved
- ○ Increased library resources included in syllabi, lectures, labs, reserves, etc.
- ○ Other: _____
- ○ Other: _____

5. What resources do you need to support your effort?

   _____
   _____

6. To whom will you report any relationships that emerge? How will those reports be structured, formatted, delivered, etc.?

   _____
   _____

7. If a relationship is established, what decisions can you make? What actions can you take?

   _____
   _____

**THINK**

How did this activity make me feel?

_____

_____

What questions do I have?

_____

_____

What do I want to learn more about?

_____

_____

What innovative ideas have emerged?

_____

_____

**TALK**

What does this mean for my library? For me, as a librarian?

_____

_____

What do we need to do differently, as a library?

_____

_____

What does this make me want to continue to do, do better, or do differently, as a librarian?

_____

_____

**TARGET**

| Action | Timeframe | Responsible Parties | Follow-Up |
|---|---|---|---|
| **Options to Consider**<br>• Contact colleague<br>• Make decision<br>• Take action<br>• Ask question<br>• Get evidence/data | **When to Do It**<br>• Today<br>• This week<br>• This month<br>• This semester<br>• This year<br>• 2-3 year plan | **Who to Involve**<br>• Students<br>• Staff<br>• Librarians<br>• Administrators<br>• Faculty | **What to Do Next**<br>After I complete this action, what's the next step? |
|  |  |  |  |
|  |  |  |  |
|  |  |  |  |
|  |  |  |  |
|  |  |  |  |

# IMPACT ON INSTITUTIONAL EFFICIENCY

## Goal

Explore the existing and potential contributions of the library to institutional efficiency.

## Why

To analyze and expand library contributions to institutional efficiency, librarians need to articulate the library's impact on this institutional focus area, plan ways to assess that impact, anticipate possible assessment results, determine a reporting and communication strategy, and brainstorm future decisions and actions.

## Directions

1. Consider possible outcomes describing library contributions to institutional efficiency.
2. Select one outcome; add details as needed.
3. Identify a target stakeholder group for this outcome.
4. Consider: What is already known or not known about this outcome?
5. Select a method or tool to assess this outcome and plan for the deployment of this tool or method.
6. Anticipate possible assessment results. (Later, replace your expected results with actual results.)
7. Brainstorm possible decisions to make and actions to take based on the results.
8. Consider: What resources are needed to support this effort?
8. Engage the **T3** process.

## Suggested Readings

Oakleaf, Megan. *The Value of Academic Libraries: A Comprehensive Research Review and Report.* Chicago: ACRL, 2010. 83–92.

Tenopir, Carol, and Donald W. King. "Perceptions of Value and Value Beyond Perceptions: Measuring the Quality and Value of Journal Article Readings." *Serials* 20, no. 3 (2007): 199–207.

## See Also

Activity #2: Stakeholders as the Heart of the Institution
Activity #44: Selecting Assessment Tools

**Possible Outcomes**

*The library will enable the stakeholder to:*

○ Save time

○ Minimize labor

○ Improve quality

○ Increase incoming funds

○ Decrease expenditures

○ Save money

○ Save money in comparison to competing information sources

○ Respond to threats

○ Minimize risks associated with bad information

○ Increase productivity

○ Gain productivity benefits associated with reading

○ Gain productivity benefits associated with adding value to reading (e.g., note-taking tools, reference management)

○ Make decisions

○ Take actions

○ Improve image or brand

○ Improve relations with other stakeholders

○ Exploit new opportunities

*For student stakeholders:*

○ Save money related to textbooks, interlibrary loan, reserves

○ Shorten time to program/degree completion

---

**Results**

What do you think the resulting data will show?

_____

_____

How will you report the results?

_____

_____

To whom will you report the results?

_____

_____

**Selected Outcome:** _____

**Target Stakeholder:** _____

What do you know so far about the degree to which this outcome is being achieved?

_____
_____

**Tools**

What method or tool might you use to assess this outcome?

○ Surveys and questionnaires
○ Experiments and control group studies
○ Interviews
○ Focus groups
○ Observations
○ Balanced scorecards
○ Ethnographic methods
○ Delphi technique
○ Critical incident technique
○ Return-on-investment analysis
○ Usage statistics
○ Tests
○ Rubrics
○ Student artifacts
○ Faculty artifacts
○ Anecdotal evidence
○ Other: _____
○ Other: _____

What would the method/tool look like?
_____
_____

What would it include?
_____
_____

How would it be enacted?
_____
_____

How might you pilot an early version?
_____
_____

What kind of data will you receive?
_____
_____

How will you analyze the data?
_____
_____

**Closing the Loop**
*Once results are "in" and reported . . .*
What decisions can you make?
_____
_____

What actions can you take?
_____
_____

What resources do you need to support this effort?
_____
_____
_____

**THINK**

How did this activity make me feel?

_____

_____

What questions do I have?

_____

_____

What do I want to learn more about?

_____

_____

What innovative ideas have emerged?

_____

_____

**TALK**

What does this mean for my library? For me, as a librarian?

_____

_____

What do we need to do differently, as a library?

_____

_____

What does this make me want to continue to do, do better, or do differently, as a librarian?

_____

_____

**TARGET**

| Action | | Timeframe | Responsible Parties | Follow-Up |
|---|---|---|---|---|
| **Options to Consider**<br>• Contact colleague<br>• Make decision<br>• Take action<br>• Ask question<br>• Get evidence/data | | **When to Do It**<br>• Today<br>• This week<br>• This month<br>• This semester<br>• This year<br>• 2-3 year plan | **Who to Involve**<br>• Students<br>• Staff<br>• Librarians<br>• Administrators<br>• Faculty | **What to Do Next**<br>After I complete this action, what's the next step? |
| | | | | |
| | | | | |
| | | | | |
| | | | | |
| | | | | |

# IMPACT ON INSTITUTIONAL PRESTIGE AND BRAND

**TAKING ACTION**

### Goal

Explore the existing and potential contributions of the library to institutional metrics and branding activities.

### Why

To analyze and expand library contributions to institutional prestige and brand, librarians need to articulate the connections between library services, expertise, and resources and this institutional focus area.

### Directions

1. Consider the metrics commonly used to gauge institutional prestige.
2. Brainstorm possible library contributions to these institutional prestige metrics.
3. Consider the marketing messages conveyed by your institution; analyze them in order to identify the core attributes of your institution's brand.
4. Identify library services, expertise, and resources that contribute to your institutional brand.
5. Brainstorm new library services, expertise, and resources that could support your institutional brand.
6. Engage the **T3** process.

### Suggested Reading

Oakleaf, Megan. *The Value of Academic Libraries: A Comprehensive Research Review and Report.* Chicago: ACRL, 2010. 52–54, 137–139.

## Institutional Prestige

1. Institutional rank is often linked to the average SAT scores of enrolled students, the graduation rate, endowment funding, and per student expenditures. How does (or could) the library contribute to these metrics?

| Prestige Metrics | Possible Library Contributions |
|---|---|
| Average SAT score of enrolled students | |
| Graduation rates | |
| Endowment funds | |
| Per student expenditures | |

2. Other institutional quality metrics include educational/professional test scores, retention rates, class size, faculty resources, and peer assessments. How does (or could) the library contribute in these areas?

| Prestige Metrics | Possible Library Contributions |
|---|---|
| Educational/professional test scores | |
| Retention rates | |
| Class size | |
| Faculty resources | |
| Peer assessments | |

## Institutional Brand

Marketing
Message
and Brand
Attributes

1. Consider your institution's marketing messages to stakeholders. What do they promote? Great research outputs? Employable students? World-class athletics? Local community support? What are the main attributes of your institutional brand?

_____

_____

_____

_____

Existing
Library
Contributions

2. What library services, expertise, or resources contribute to the institutional brand? Has your library won awards? Does it offer unique or local interest collections? Are there programs that encourage local community involvement?

_____

_____

_____

_____

New or
Improved
Library
Contributions

3. What library services, expertise, or resources could contribute to the institutional brand if the library did something differently or better?

_____

_____

_____

_____

**THINK**

How did this activity make me feel?

_____

_____

What questions do I have?

_____

_____

What do I want to learn more about?

_____

_____

What innovative ideas have emerged?

_____

_____

**TALK**

What does this mean for my library? For me, as a librarian?

_____

_____

What do we need to do differently, as a library?

_____

_____

What does this make me want to continue to do, do better, or do differently, as a librarian?

_____

_____

**TARGET**

| Action | Timeframe | Responsible Parties | Follow-Up |
|---|---|---|---|
| **Options to Consider**<br>• Contact colleague<br>• Make decision<br>• Take action<br>• Ask question<br>• Get evidence/data | **When to Do It**<br>• Today<br>• This week<br>• This month<br>• This semester<br>• This year<br>• 2-3 year plan | **Who to Involve**<br>• Students<br>• Staff<br>• Librarians<br>• Administrators<br>• Faculty | **What to Do Next**<br>After I complete this action, what's the next step? |
|  |  |  |  |
|  |  |  |  |
|  |  |  |  |
|  |  |  |  |
|  |  |  |  |

# THINKING IMPACT THROUGH

## Goal
Envision the steps required to link institutional focus areas and library services, expertise, or resources using supporting evidence.

## Why
To gain a macro-level perspective, librarians need to envision and anticipate the steps associated with connecting institutional focus areas to library services and resources.

## Directions
1. Select an institutional focus area.
2. Work through Steps #1–3 in in the flowchart.
3. Select a library service or resource in Step #4.
4. Work through Steps #5–6.
5. Respond to the Reflection Questions.
6. Engage the **T3** process.

## See Also
Activity #1: Institutional Focus Areas
Activity #25: Assessment Fears, Challenges, and Barriers
Activity #36: Keeping Impact Simple

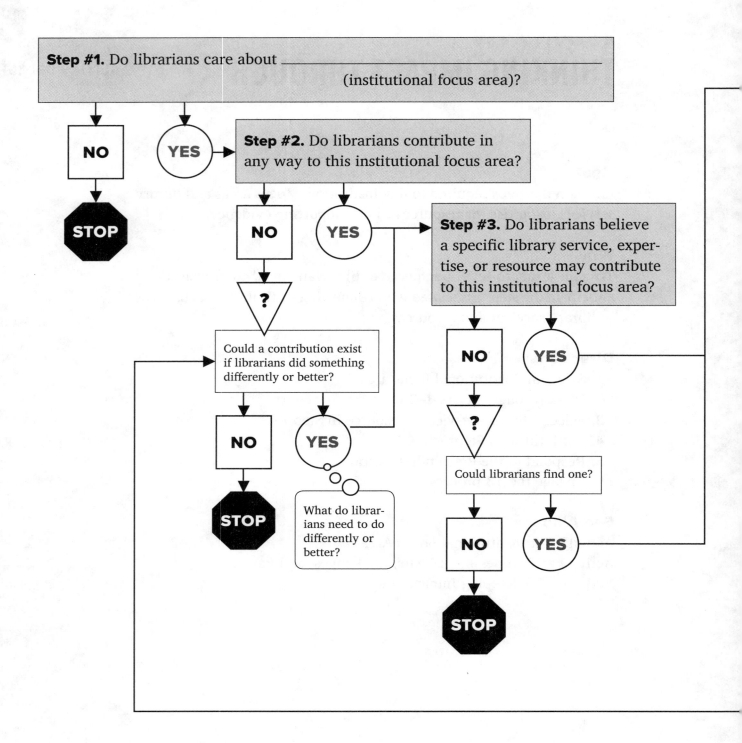

**Reflection Questions:**

1. At what point in this process might you or your library encounter challenges?

   _____

   _____

   _____

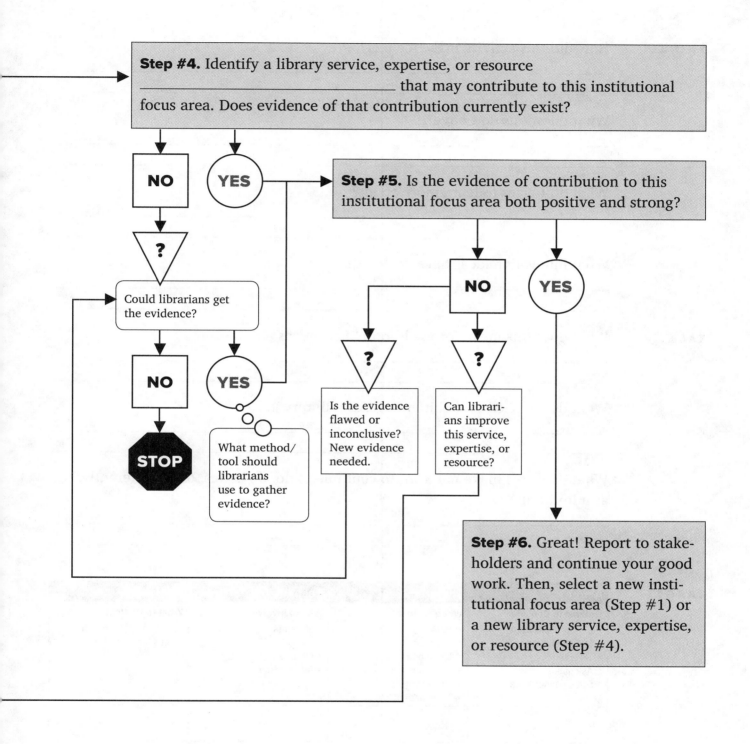

2. How might you overcome these challenges?

_____

_____

_____

**THINK**

How did this activity make me feel?

_____

_____

What questions do I have?

_____

_____

What do I want to learn more about?

_____

_____

What innovative ideas have emerged?

_____

_____

**TALK**

What does this mean for my library? For me, as a librarian?

_____

_____

What do we need to do differently, as a library?

_____

_____

What does this make me want to continue to do, do better, or do differently, as a librarian?

_____

_____

**TARGET**

| Action | Timeframe | Responsible Parties | Follow-Up |
|---|---|---|---|
| **Options to Consider**<br>• Contact colleague<br>• Make decision<br>• Take action<br>• Ask question<br>• Get evidence/data | **When to Do It**<br>• Today<br>• This week<br>• This month<br>• This semester<br>• This year<br>• 2-3 year plan | **Who to Involve**<br>• Students<br>• Staff<br>• Librarians<br>• Administrators<br>• Faculty | **What to Do Next**<br>After I complete this action, what's the next step? |
| | | | |
| | | | |
| | | | |
| | | | |
| | | | |

ACTIVITY #36
# KEEPING IMPACT SIMPLE

GETTING ORGANIZED

## Goal
Articulate library impact clearly and succinctly.

## Why
To communicate and increase their impact, librarians need to explain library impact on stakeholders, including evidence of impact and ideas for improvements that will expand library impact.

## Directions
1. Respond to the Reflection Questions.
2. Draft simple statements describing library impact, evidence, and anticipated change to stakeholders.
3. Engage the **T3** process.

## See Also
Activity #1: Institutional Focus Areas
Activity #2: Stakeholders as the Heart of the Institution
Activity #35: Thinking Impact Through

## Reflection Questions

1. In the context of institutional focus areas, what impact does the library (or specific library services, expertise, or resources) make on its stakeholders?

   _____

   _____

   _____

   _____

2. Does evidence of the impact exist?

   _____

   _____

   _____

   _____

3. Is that evidence shared with stakeholders?

   _____

   _____

   _____

4. In the context of institutional focus areas, what impact could the library (or specific library services, expertise, or resources) make on its stakeholders if it did something differently or better?

   _____

   _____

   _____

5. What is that "something" that could be done differently or better?

   _____

   _____

   _____

## Library Impact, Evidence, and Anticipated Change

Describe clearly and succinctly.

_____

_____

_____

_____

_____

_____

_____

_____

_____

_____

_____

_____

_____

_____

_____

_____

_____

**THINK**

How did this activity make me feel?

_____

_____

What questions do I have?

_____

_____

What do I want to learn more about?

_____

_____

What innovative ideas have emerged?

_____

_____

**TALK**

What does this mean for my library? For me, as a librarian?

_____

_____

What do we need to do differently, as a library?

_____

_____

What does this make me want to continue to do, do better, or do differently, as a librarian?

_____

_____

**TARGET**

| Action | Timeframe | Responsible Parties | Follow-Up |
|---|---|---|---|
| **Options to Consider**<br>• Contact colleague<br>• Make decision<br>• Take action<br>• Ask question<br>• Get evidence/data | **When to Do It**<br>• Today<br>• This week<br>• This month<br>• This semester<br>• This year<br>• 2-3 year plan | **Who to Involve**<br>• Students<br>• Staff<br>• Librarians<br>• Administrators<br>• Faculty | **What to Do Next**<br>After I complete this action, what's the next step? |
|  |  |  |  |
|  |  |  |  |
|  |  |  |  |
|  |  |  |  |
|  |  |  |  |

ACTIVITY #37
# PLANNING FOR ASSESSMENT

GETTING ORGANIZED

### Goal
Select components to include in library assessment plans.

### Why
To ensure effective assessment practices, librarians need to develop assessment plans including overview statements, strategic document links, support structures, data policies, "closing the loop" plans, resources, partners, and detailed outcome information.

### Directions
1. Consider the components of library assessment plans.
2. Check off desirable components for your new or existing library assessment plan.
3. Engage the **T3** process.

### Suggested Reading
Oakleaf, Megan. "Writing Information Literacy Assessment Plans: A Guide to Best Practice." *Communications in Information Literacy*. 3(2). 2010.

## Assessment Plan Components

### Overview
○ Purpose
○ Guiding theories
○ Guiding values
○ Links to institutional focus areas

### Links to strategic documents
○ Mission (library, institutional)
○ Vision (library, institutional)
○ Standards (library associations, accrediting agencies)
○ Strategic plans (library, institutional)
○ Strategic priorities (library, institutional)
○ Strategic needs (library, institutional)

### Support structures
○ Professional development/capacity building
○ Advisors/consultants
○ Committees/coordinators

### Data policies
○ Human subjects/ethics
○ Populations/sampling
○ Elicitation/gathering/ input/collection
○ Tools/systems
○ Organization
○ Analysis
○ Interpretation
○ Access/permissions
○ Transparency
○ Reporting plans
○ Communication plans
○ Dissemination plans

### Closing the loop
○ Results
○ Decision-making uses
○ Action-taking uses
○ Impacts/improvements
○ Budgetary changes
○ Assessment changes

### Resources
○ Budgets
○ Incentives
○ Spaces/facilities

**Partners/collaborators/personnel**
- ⭕ Library
- ⭕ Stakeholders
- ⭕ Institution
- ⭕ Accrediting agencies

**Glossary of terms**

**Outcomes**
- ⭕ Service outcomes
- ⭕ Resource outcomes
- ⭕ Development outcomes
- ⭕ Learning outcomes

- ⭕ Other: _____
- ⭕ Other: _____

**For each outcome**
- ⭕ What is known/not known about the outcome
- ⭕ Criteria for success/how assessors will know the outcome has been met
- ⭕ Target populations
- ⭕ Opportunities for assessments
- ⭕ Curriculum maps
- ⭕ Connections to institutional/program/department/unit outcomes
- ⭕ Methods/tools/measures
- ⭕ Multiple measure recommendations
- ⭕ Pilot recommendations
- ⭕ Responsible parties
- ⭕ Interested parties/stakeholders
- ⭕ Tasks/workflows
- ⭕ Timelines/schedules
- ⭕ Anticipated results/metrics
- ⭕ Actual results/metrics
- ⭕ Decision-making, action-taking indicators
- ⭕ Closing the loop/decisions made/actions taken

**THINK**

How did this activity make me feel?

_____

_____

What questions do I have?

_____

_____

What do I want to learn more about?

_____

_____

What innovative ideas have emerged?

_____

_____

**TALK**

What does this mean for my library? For me, as a librarian?

_____

_____

What do we need to do differently, as a library?

_____

_____

What does this make me want to continue to do, do better, or do differently, as a librarian?

_____

_____

**TARGET**

| Action | | Timeframe | Responsible Parties | Follow-Up |
|---|---|---|---|---|
| **Options to Consider**<br>• Contact colleague<br>• Make decision<br>• Take action<br>• Ask question<br>• Get evidence/data | | **When to Do It**<br>• Today<br>• This week<br>• This month<br>• This semester<br>• This year<br>• 2-3 year plan | **Who to Involve**<br>• Students<br>• Staff<br>• Librarians<br>• Administrators<br>• Faculty | **What to Do Next**<br>After I complete this action, what's the next step? |
| | | | | |
| | | | | |
| | | | | |
| | | | | |
| | | | | |

# GATHERING LIBRARY IMPACT LITERATURE

## Goal

Collect "best practice" and research literature about library contributions to institutional focus areas.

## Why

To change practice, librarians need to engage in reading and producing literature about library contributions to institutional focus areas.

## Directions

1. Consider your information needs, hypotheses, or research questions.
2. Brainstorm search terms and strategies.
3. Consider, select, and search information sources.
4. Apply evaluative criteria to select relevant literature.
5. Read literature critically to identify inspiring ideas, models to emulate, useful methods and tools, and interesting results.
6. Engage the **T3** process.

## Suggested Readings

Oakleaf, Megan. *The Value of Academic Libraries: A Comprehensive Research Review and Report.* Chicago: ACRL, 2010. 25.

Oakleaf, Megan. "What's the Value of an Academic Library? The Development of the Value of Academic Libraries Comprehensive Research Review and Report." *Australian Academic and Research Libraries.* 2011. 1–13.

## Information Need/Hypothesis/Research Question

_____

_____

_____

## Useful Search Terms

○ Evaluation
○ Assessment
○ Value
○ Impact
○ Outcome assessment
○ College and university libraries
○ Academic libraries
○ Community college libraries
○ Research libraries
○ Recruitment
○ Retention
○ College dropouts
○ Learning
○ Authentic assessment
○ Academic achievement
○ Performance evaluation

○ Grade point average
○ Engagement
○ Student participation
○ Student surveys
○ College teachers
○ Faculty
○ Grants
○ Research
○ Action research
○ Experimental design
○ Decision-making
○ Program effectiveness
○ Accreditation
○ Educational accountability
○ Other: _____
○ Other: _____

## Information Sources

○ Articles from library databases (Library Literature, LISA, LISTA, etc.)
○ Articles from higher education databases (Education Source, ERIC, Education Research Complete, etc.)
○ Books/book chapters
○ Conference presentations/proceedings
○ Listservs/blogs/wikis/forums
○ Data/statistical sources
○ White papers/preprints/gray literature
○ Word of mouth
○ Open web
○ Citation tracing
○ Other: _____
○ Other: _____

## Evaluation Criteria

○ Focuses on library contributions to institutional focus areas

○ Describes institutional focus areas of interest to librarians, although libraries may not be specifically mentioned

○ Includes research or assessment models, methods, tools, or results usable or related to library contributions to institutional focus areas

○ Depicts best practices in library contributions to institutional focus areas

○ Offers a compelling argument supporting library contributions to institutional focus areas

○ Includes a thorough literature review supporting library contributions to institutional focus areas

○ Provides accurate and detailed analysis of results showing library contributions to institutional focus areas

○ Explains conclusions about library contributions to institutional focus areas clearly and logically

○ States all limitations and their impact on conclusions about library contributions to institutional focus areas

## Usable Inspirations, Models, Methods, Tools, or Results

_____

_____

_____

_____

_____

_____

_____

_____

_____

_____

_____

_____

**THINK**

How did this activity make me feel?

_____

_____

What questions do I have?

_____

_____

What do I want to learn more about?

_____

_____

What innovative ideas have emerged?

_____

_____

**TALK**

What does this mean for my library? For me, as a librarian?

_____

_____

What do we need to do differently, as a library?

_____

_____

What does this make me want to continue to do, do better, or do differently, as a librarian?

_____

_____

**TARGET**

| Action | Timeframe | Responsible Parties | Follow-Up |
|---|---|---|---|
| **Options to Consider** <br> • Contact colleague <br> • Make decision <br> • Take action <br> • Ask question <br> • Get evidence/data | **When to Do It** <br> • Today <br> • This week <br> • This month <br> • This semester <br> • This year <br> • 2-3 year plan | **Who to Involve** <br> • Students <br> • Staff <br> • Librarians <br> • Administrators <br> • Faculty | **What to Do Next** <br> After I complete this action, what's the next step? |
|  |  |  |  |
|  |  |  |  |
|  |  |  |  |
|  |  |  |  |
|  |  |  |  |

# ENGAGING THE ASSESSMENT CYCLE

## Goal

Clarify connections between library services, expertise, and resources, outcomes of significance to institutional focus areas, evidence resulting from assessment efforts, and decisions or actions resulting from that evidence.

## Why

To demonstrate to stakeholders that library services, expertise, and resources contribute to institutional focus areas, librarians need to align them with outcomes as well as assessment measures and results that provide evidence of reflective practice, continuous improvement, and "closing the loop."

## Directions

1. Enter a library service, expertise, or resource in the blank labeled, "This is who we are."
2. List the outcomes the service, expertise, or resource seeks to achieve, including library-defined outcomes, campus (e.g., departmental, unit, program, strategic, administrative, general education) outcomes, professional outcomes, etc.
3. Describe the activities, techniques, and strategies librarians employ to enable the library service, expertise, or resource to achieve its outcomes.
4. Identify (or suggest) the methods and tools employed to assess the library service or resource.
5. State (or hypothesize) the resulting assessment evidence/data that reveals the degree to which the library service, expertise, or resource has achieved its outcomes.
6. Record (or imagine) what decisions or actions might be taken based on assessment evidence/data.
7. Engage the **T3** process.

### Suggested Reading

Oakleaf, Megan. "The Information Literacy Instruction Assessment
 Cycle: A Guide for Increasing Student Learning and Improving
 Librarian Instructional Skills." *Journal of Documentation.* 65(4).
 2009. 539–560.

### See Also

Activity #9: Institutional Program Review and Accreditation Audit
Activity #10: Institutional Learning Outcome Audit

> " This is who we are; these are the skills and competencies that we strive to instill in students; these programs and efforts are how we do that; and these data illustrate the sum of our efforts."
>
> —RICHARD KEELING

**This is who we are:**

_____

_____

_____

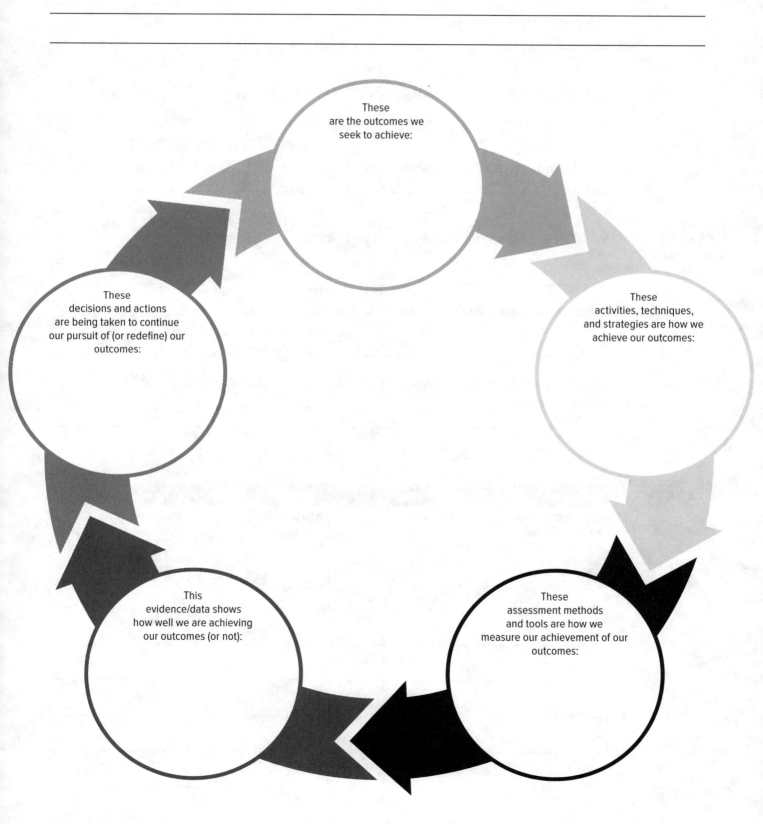

These
are the outcomes we
seek to achieve:

These
activities, techniques,
and strategies are how we
achieve our outcomes:

These
decisions and actions
are being taken to continue
our pursuit of (or redefine) our
outcomes:

These
assessment methods
and tools are how we
measure our achievement of our
outcomes:

This
evidence/data shows
how well we are achieving
our outcomes (or not):

**THINK**     How did this activity make me feel?

_____

_____

What questions do I have?

_____

_____

What do I want to learn more about?

_____

_____

What innovative ideas have emerged?

_____

_____

**TALK**      What does this mean for my library? For me, as a librarian?

_____

_____

What do we need to do differently, as a library?

_____

_____

What does this make me want to continue to do, do better, or do differently, as a librarian?

_____

_____

**TARGET**

| Action | | Timeframe | Responsible Parties | Follow-Up |
|---|---|---|---|---|
| **Options to Consider**<br>• Contact colleague<br>• Make decision<br>• Take action<br>• Ask question<br>• Get evidence/data | | **When to Do It**<br>• Today<br>• This week<br>• This month<br>• This semester<br>• This year<br>• 2-3 year plan | **Who to Involve**<br>• Students<br>• Staff<br>• Librarians<br>• Administrators<br>• Faculty | **What to Do Next**<br>After I complete this action, what's the next step? |
| | | | | |
| | | | | |
| | | | | |
| | | | | |
| | | | | |

# PREPARING A CONTINUOUS ASSESSMENT TIMELINE

## Goal

Plan a continuous assessment timeline for demonstrating library contributions to institutional focus areas.

## Why

To undertake the assessment required to demonstrate library contributions to institutional focus areas, librarians need to create continuous assessment timelines to guide their assessment activities.

## Directions

1. Consider the cycles that guide library assessment: the assessment cycle, evidence-based practice, reflective practice, pragmatism, and information literacy.
2. Consider these cycles as guides for continuous assessment timelines.
3. Select an institutional focus area.
4. Develop a continuous assessment timeline for this institutional focus area. List actions to take, responsible parties, and target dates for completion.
5. Engage the **T3** process.

## Suggested Readings

Oakleaf, Megan. "Are They Learning? Are We? Learning and the Academic Library." *Library Quarterly*. 81(1). 2011. 61–82.

Oakleaf, Megan. "The Information Literacy Instruction Assessment Cycle: A Guide for Increasing Student Learning and Improving Librarian Instructional Skills." *Journal of Documentation*. 65(4). 2009. 539–560.

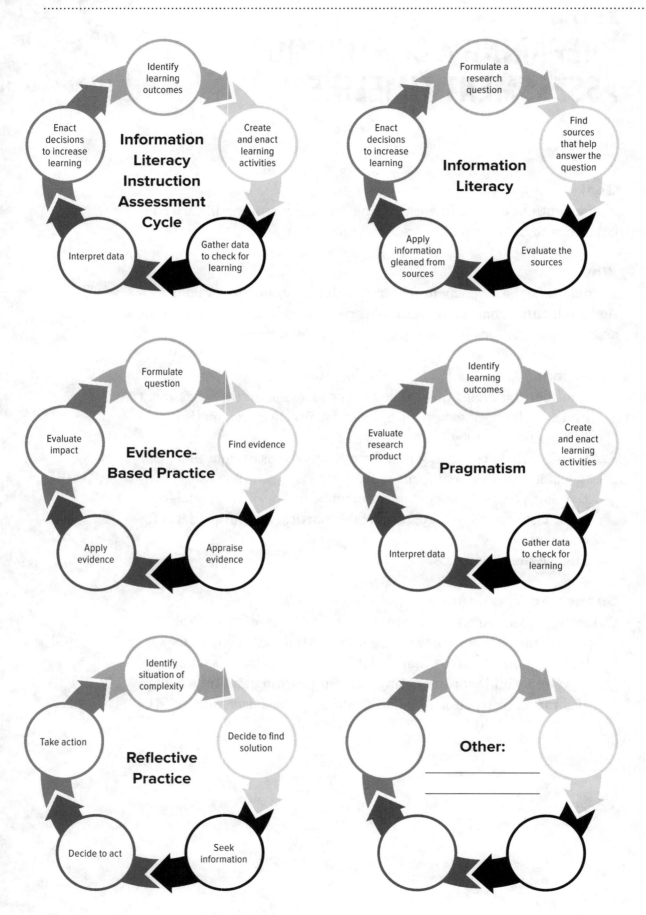

## Institutional Focus Area: _____

Action:
_____

Responsible Parties:
_____

Target for Completion:
_____

Action:
_____

Responsible Parties:
_____

Target for Completion:
_____

Action:
_____

Responsible Parties:
_____

Target for Completion:
_____

Action:
_____

Responsible Parties:
_____

Target for Completion:
_____

Action:
_____

Responsible Parties:
_____

Target for Completion:
_____

**THINK**

How did this activity make me feel?

_____

_____

What questions do I have?

_____

_____

What do I want to learn more about?

_____

_____

What innovative ideas have emerged?

_____

_____

**TALK**

What does this mean for my library? For me, as a librarian?

_____

_____

What do we need to do differently, as a library?

_____

_____

What does this make me want to continue to do, do better, or do differently, as a librarian?

_____

_____

**TARGET**

| Action | Timeframe | Responsible Parties | Follow-Up |
|---|---|---|---|
| **Options to Consider**<br>• Contact colleague<br>• Make decision<br>• Take action<br>• Ask question<br>• Get evidence/data | **When to Do It**<br>• Today<br>• This week<br>• This month<br>• This semester<br>• This year<br>• 2-3 year plan | **Who to Involve**<br>• Students<br>• Staff<br>• Librarians<br>• Administrators<br>• Faculty | **What to Do Next**<br>After I complete this action, what's the next step? |
| | | | |
| | | | |
| | | | |
| | | | |
| | | | |

# INVOLVING THE ENTIRE LIBRARY ORGANIZATION

### Goal

Align the efforts of all library organizational units toward developing, assessing, and communicating library service, expertise, and resource contributions to institutional focus areas.

### Why

To operate efficiently, librarians need to distribute responsibilities for contributing to institutional focus areas across all organizational units.

### Directions

1. Select an institutional focus area.
2. Consider the library services, expertise, and resources that contribute to that institutional focus area.
3. Work through each organizational unit. In what way is each organizational unit responsible for connecting library services, expertise, and resources to the institutional focus area?
4. Respond to the Reflection Questions.
5. Engage the **T3** process.

### See Also

Activity #1: Institutional Focus Areas
Activity #26: Library Impact Map

## Institutional Focus Area: _____

## Contributing Library Services, Expertise, and Resources: _____

| ORGANIZATIONAL UNIT | How does this organizational unit contribute to this institutional focus area? | How can this organizational unit assess contributions to this focus area? |
| --- | --- | --- |
| Professional associations | | |
| Consortia | | |
| Libraries | | |
| Senior library administrators/leaders | | |
| Library departments/units | | |
| Library department/unit heads | | |
| Front-line librarians | | |
| Library staff | | |
| Student employees | | |
| Friends of the library | | |
| Library advisory committees | | |
| Library volunteers | | |
| Other: | | |
| Other: | | |

| How can this organizational unit increase contributions to this institutional focus area by doing something differently or better? | How can this organizational unit communicate contributions to this institutional focus area to stakeholders? |
| --- | --- |
| | |
| | |
| | |
| | |
| | |
| | |
| | |
| | |
| | |
| | |
| | |

**THINK**

How did this activity make me feel?

_____

_____

What questions do I have?

_____

_____

What do I want to learn more about?

_____

_____

What innovative ideas have emerged?

_____

_____

**TALK**

What does this mean for my library? For me, as a librarian?

_____

_____

What do we need to do differently, as a library?

_____

_____

What does this make me want to continue to do, do better, or do differently, as a librarian?

_____

_____

**TARGET**

| Action | | Timeframe | Responsible Parties | Follow-Up |
|---|---|---|---|---|
| **Options to Consider**<br>• Contact colleague<br>• Make decision<br>• Take action<br>• Ask question<br>• Get evidence/data | | **When to Do It**<br>• Today<br>• This week<br>• This month<br>• This semester<br>• This year<br>• 2-3 year plan | **Who to Involve**<br>• Students<br>• Staff<br>• Librarians<br>• Administrators<br>• Faculty | **What to Do Next**<br>After I complete this action, what's the next step? |
| | | | | |
| | | | | |
| | | | | |
| | | | | |
| | | | | |

ACTIVITY #42

# APPROACHING INSTITUTIONAL RESEARCH COLLABORATIONS

**TAKING ACTION**

### Goal

Prepare to collaborate with institutional research professionals to explore the library's impact on individuals.

### Why

To ascertain the library's impact on individuals, librarians may need to collaborate with institutional research professionals in order to investigate multiple or institution-level data sets.

### Directions

1. Once ideas for research or assessments involving multiple or institution-level data sets emerge, identify institutional research professionals at your institution.
2. Consider your research or assessment interest. Write that interest in the form of a research question or hypothesis.
3. Consider the ways you will use the results of your research or assessment. What benefits do you expect to emerge?
4. Consider your stakeholders. Which stakeholders will be interested in your research or assessment?
5. Consider the data you need to investigate your research question or hypothesis. What format is it in? How is it housed? What analyses do you plan to use? What is your timeframe?
6. Engage the **T3** process.

### See Also

Activity #2: Stakeholders as the Heart of the Institution
Activity #43: Approaching Human Subjects Research

> ❝ The library 'exists to benefit the students of the educational institution as individuals.'
>
> —RICHARD KEELING

**171**

1. What is your research question or hypothesis?

_____

_____

_____

_____

2. How do you intend to use your results?

_____

_____

_____

_____

3. What benefits do you anticipate will come from your results?

_____

_____

_____

_____

4. What stakeholder groups will be interested in your results? Can institutional researchers use your results? How?

_____

_____

_____

_____

5. What data do you need to investigate your research question or hypothesis?

_____

_____

_____

_____

6. What format is the data in? What format do you need it to be in?

_____

_____

_____

_____

7. What systems house the data? If the data is housed in multiple systems, do the systems "talk" to each other?

_____

_____

_____

_____

8. What kinds of analysis do you intend to pursue? Do you have the resources to run these analyses or will you require assistance?

_____

_____

_____

_____

9. What is the timeframe? What deadlines apply?

_____

_____

_____

_____

10. Do you have human subjects research approval?

_____

_____

_____

**THINK**

How did this activity make me feel?

_____

_____

What questions do I have?

_____

_____

What do I want to learn more about?

_____

_____

What innovative ideas have emerged?

_____

_____

**TALK**

What does this mean for my library? For me, as a librarian?

_____

_____

What do we need to do differently, as a library?

_____

_____

What does this make me want to continue to do, do better, or do differently, as a librarian?

_____

_____

**TARGET**

| Action | Timeframe | Responsible Parties | Follow-Up |
|---|---|---|---|
| **Options to Consider** | **When to Do It** | **Who to Involve** | **What to Do Next** |
| • Contact colleague<br>• Make decision<br>• Take action<br>• Ask question<br>• Get evidence/data | • Today<br>• This week<br>• This month<br>• This semester<br>• This year<br>• 2-3 year plan | • Students<br>• Staff<br>• Librarians<br>• Administrators<br>• Faculty | After I complete this action, what's the next step? |
| | | | |
| | | | |
| | | | |
| | | | |
| | | | |

# APPROACHING HUMAN SUBJECTS RESEARCH

**TAKING ACTION**

## Goal

Prepare to engage in research or assessment involving human subjects.

## Why

To investigate the library's impact on individuals, librarians may need to conduct research or assessment that requires institutional review board approval.

## Directions

1. Once ideas for research or assessment involving human subjects emerge, locate and read information on the institutional review board process.
2. Consider the characteristics of each review category; add any that are missing. What review category matches your research or assessment?
3. Consider the elements of review applications, as well as other application issues.
4. Optional: Schedule an appointment with a human subjects research professional to ask questions and elicit advice and recommendations.
5. Engage the **T3** process.

## Suggested Reading

Oakleaf, Megan. *The Value of Academic Libraries: A Comprehensive Research Review and Report.* Chicago: ACRL, 2010. 43, 94–97.

## See Also

Activity #2: Stakeholders as the Heart of the Institution

> "Until libraries know that student #5 with major A has downloaded B number of articles from database C, checked out D number of books, participated in E workshops and online tutorials, and completed courses F, G, and H, libraries cannot correlate any of those student information behaviors with attainment of other outcomes. Until librarians do that, they will be blocked in many of their efforts to demonstrate value." —MEGAN OAKLEAF

1. At your institution, what type of research or assessment falls into each of the following review categories?

| Exempt Review | ○ Anonymous surveys<br>○ Existing public data<br>○ Research in established or commonly accepted education settings involving normal educational practices<br>○ Other:<br>○ Other: |
|---|---|
| Expedited Review | ○ No more than minimal risk<br>○ Other:<br>○ Other:<br>○ Other: |
| Full Review | ○ Greater than minimal risk<br>○ Other:<br>○ Other:<br>○ Other: |
| Special Population Review | ○ Children<br>○ Prisoners<br>○ Cognitively impaired persons<br>○ Other:<br>○ Other: |

2. Which review category does your research or assessment fall into?
   ○ Exempt   ○ Expedited   ○ Full   ○ Special Population   ○ Other

3. Do you plan to publish or present your results? How does that impact the review category for your research or assessment?

4. Based on the review category, what components do you need to include in your review application?

   ○ Research purpose or rationale
   ○ Research questions or hypotheses
   ○ Research methods
   ○ Research qualifications
   ○ Participant characteristics
   ○ Participant recruitment
   ○ Data collection and storage
   ○ Privacy and confidentiality precautions
   ○ Risks to participants
   ○ Strategies to manage/ minimize risks
   ○ Benefits to participants
   ○ Benefits to society
   ○ Ways that benefits outweigh risks

   ○ Informed consent
   ○ Statement of research study
   ○ Research purpose
   ○ Research procedures
   ○ Duration of involvement
   ○ Voluntary participation and right to withdraw without penalty
   ○ Right to confidentiality
   ○ Risks and benefits
   ○ Contact information
   ○ Other: _____
   ○ Other: _____

5. How long should you allow for the review process?

_____

_____

_____

6. Do you need to complete any special training?

_____

_____

_____

7. Are there example documents you can use as models?

_____

_____

_____

8. What are common mistakes made in review applications?

_____

_____

_____

9. Who can answer questions about the review process?

_____

_____

_____

10. Once your application is approved, what other rules and procedures do you need to follow?

_____

_____

_____

**THINK**  How did this activity make me feel?

_____

_____

What questions do I have?

_____

_____

What do I want to learn more about?

_____

_____

What innovative ideas have emerged?

_____

_____

**TALK**  What does this mean for my library? For me, as a librarian?

_____

_____

What do we need to do differently, as a library?

_____

_____

What does this make me want to continue to do, do better, or do differently, as a librarian?

_____

_____

**TARGET**

| Action | Timeframe | Responsible Parties | Follow-Up |
|---|---|---|---|
| **Options to Consider**<br>• Contact colleague<br>• Make decision<br>• Take action<br>• Ask question<br>• Get evidence/data | **When to Do It**<br>• Today<br>• This week<br>• This month<br>• This semester<br>• This year<br>• 2-3 year plan | **Who to Involve**<br>• Students<br>• Staff<br>• Librarians<br>• Administrators<br>• Faculty | **What to Do Next**<br>After I complete this action, what's the next step? |
|  |  |  |  |
|  |  |  |  |
|  |  |  |  |
|  |  |  |  |
|  |  |  |  |

## ACTIVITY #44
# SELECTING ASSESSMENT TOOLS

**TAKING ACTION**

### Goal
Select tools for assessment or research projects.

### Why
In order to ensure rigorous investigations of library contributions to institutional focus areas, librarians need to identify, evaluate, and determine the most appropriate assessment tools.

### Directions
1. Consider the tools and artifacts that can be used for assessment and research.
2. Check off tools and artifacts that are feasible, convey useful information, and fit your assessment or research goals and resources.
3. Respond to the Reflection Questions.
4. Engage the **T3** process.

### Suggested Readings

Matthews, Joseph R. *The Evaluation and Measurement of Library Services*. Westport, CT: Libraries Unlimited, 2007.

Oakleaf, Megan. "Dangers and Opportunities: A Conceptual Map of Information Literacy Assessment Tools." *portal: Libraries and the Academy*. 8(3). 2008. 233–253.

Oakleaf, Megan. *The Value of Academic Libraries: A Comprehensive Research Review and Report*. Chicago: ACRL, 2010. 60–65.

Oakleaf, Megan. "Writing Information Literacy Assessment Plans: A Guide to Best Practice." *Communications in Information Literacy*. 3(2). 2010.

Oakleaf, Megan and Neal Kaske. "Guiding Questions for Assessing Information Literacy in Higher Education." *portal: Libraries and the Academy*. 9(2). 2009. 273–286.

## Tools

- ❍ Surveys and questionnaires
- ❍ Experiments and control group studies
- ❍ Interviews
- ❍ Focus groups
- ❍ Observation
- ❍ Delphi technique
- ❍ Balanced scorecard
- ❍ Ethnographic methods
- ❍ Critical incident technique
- ❍ Return-on-investment analysis
  - ❍ Consumer surplus
  - ❍ Contingent valuation
  - ❍ Economic benefit
  - ❍ Library valuation
  - ❍ Investment in access
- ❍ Other: _____
- ❍ Other: _____

## Artifacts

- ❍ Institutional assessment reports
- ❍ Accreditation documents
- ❍ Strategic documents
- ❍ Benchmarks
- ❍ Usage statistics
- ❍ Transaction logs
- ❍ Faculty research products
- ❍ Student course assignments
- ❍ Tests
- ❍ Research logs
- ❍ Rubrics
- ❍ Portfolios
- ❍ Institution-level information systems
- ❍ Integrated library systems
- ❍ Vendor data
- ❍ Anecdotes
- ❍ Other: _____
- ❍ Other: _____

## Reflection Questions

1. Who may already have the evidence/data you could collect with these tools and artifacts?

   _____

   _____

   _____

   _____

   _____

   _____

   _____

2. What are the advantages and disadvantages of these tools and artifacts?

| TOOL | ADVANTAGES | DISADVANTAGES |
|---|---|---|
|  |  |  |
|  |  |  |
|  |  |  |
|  |  |  |
|  |  |  |
|  |  |  |

3. Which tools and artifacts would be complementary in a triangulated or mixed methods study?

_____

_____

_____

_____

_____

_____

**THINK**

How did this activity make me feel?

_____

_____

What questions do I have?

_____

_____

What do I want to learn more about?

_____

_____

What innovative ideas have emerged?

_____

_____

**TALK**

What does this mean for my library? For me, as a librarian?

_____

_____

What do we need to do differently, as a library?

_____

_____

What does this make me want to continue to do, do better, or do differently, as a librarian?

_____

_____

**TARGET**

| Action | Timeframe | Responsible Parties | Follow-Up |
|---|---|---|---|
| **Options to Consider**<br>• Contact colleague<br>• Make decision<br>• Take action<br>• Ask question<br>• Get evidence/data | **When to Do It**<br>• Today<br>• This week<br>• This month<br>• This semester<br>• This year<br>• 2-3 year plan | **Who to Involve**<br>• Students<br>• Staff<br>• Librarians<br>• Administrators<br>• Faculty | **What to Do Next**<br>After I complete this action, what's the next step? |
| | | | |
| | | | |
| | | | |
| | | | |
| | | | |

# CHOOSING ASSESSMENT OR RESEARCH

### Goal
Select an approach to investigations of library contributions to institutional focus areas.

### Why
In order to design rigorous investigations of library contributions to institutional focus areas, librarians need to determine the most appropriate paradigm: assessment or research.

### Directions
1. Consider the attributes of assessment projects and research projects.
2. Check off desirable attributes.
3. Respond to the Reflection Questions.
4. Engage the **T3** process.

### Suggested Reading
Oakleaf, Megan. *The Value of Academic Libraries: A Comprehensive Research Review and Report.* Chicago: ACRL, 2010. 30–32.

| Assessment | vs. | Research |
|---|---|---|

**Assessment**

○ Gain evidence/data for decision-making or action-taking

○ Be organizationally transparent

○ Communicate with stakeholders

○ Foster improvement

○ Increase efficiency

○ Articulate effectiveness

○ Demonstrate accountability

○ Engage in reflection and reflective practice

○ Facilitate improvement

○ Change the status quo

○ Advocate for increased resources

○ Observe change

○ Tolerate, but document, flaws in assessment processes

**Research**

○ Prove or disprove hypotheses

○ Investigate correlative or causative relationships among variables

○ Start over if flaws in research design interfere

## Reflection Questions

1. Which approach fits your goals? Why?

   _____

   _____

   _____

   _____

   _____

2. Which approach fits your resources (time, money, skills)? Explain.

   _____

   _____

   _____

   _____

   _____

3. What do you give up when you choose one approach over the other?

   _____

   _____

   _____

   _____

   _____

**THINK**

How did this activity make me feel?

_____

_____

What questions do I have?

_____

_____

What do I want to learn more about?

_____

_____

What innovative ideas have emerged?

_____

_____

**TALK**

What does this mean for my library? For me, as a librarian?

_____

_____

What do we need to do differently, as a library?

_____

_____

What does this make me want to continue to do, do better, or do differently, as a librarian?

_____

_____

**TARGET**

| Action | Timeframe | Responsible Parties | Follow-Up |
|---|---|---|---|
| **Options to Consider** <br> • Contact colleague <br> • Make decision <br> • Take action <br> • Ask question <br> • Get evidence/data | **When to Do It** <br> • Today <br> • This week <br> • This month <br> • This semester <br> • This year <br> • 2-3 year plan | **Who to Involve** <br> • Students <br> • Staff <br> • Librarians <br> • Administrators <br> • Faculty | **What to Do Next** <br> After I complete this action, what's the next step? |
|  |  |  |  |
|  |  |  |  |
|  |  |  |  |
|  |  |  |  |
|  |  |  |  |

# PLANNING PARTNERSHIPS

**TAKING ACTION**

## Goal
Prepare to approach potential partners in the contribution to institutional focus areas.

## Why
To engage others in the library's contribution to institutional focus areas, librarians need to identify partners and develop partnerships.

## Directions
1. Consider list of the partners; add any that are missing.
2. Select partners and enter them in the left column.
3. Work through the chart one partner at a time.
4. Consider the components of an "elevator speech."
5. Draft an elevator speech to deliver to a partner.
6. Practice your speech independently or with a colleague.
7. Engage the **T3** process.

## See Also
Activity #26: Library Impact Map

| PARTNER | What institutional focus areas does this partner care about? | What services, expertise, or resources does the library offer that contribute to these institutional focus areas? |
|---|---|---|
|  |  |  |
|  |  |  |
|  |  |  |
|  |  |  |
|  |  |  |
|  |  |  |

## Partners

- ○ Office of institutional research or educational assessment
- ○ Office of research, sponsored programs, or technology transfer
- ○ Student affairs professionals
- ○ Faculty
- ○ Academic advisors
- ○ Program review committee
- ○ Center for teaching and learning
- ○ Academic support services
- ○ Senior institutional leaders
- ○ Accreditors
- ○ Professional associations
- ○ Funding agencies
- ○ Other: _____
- ○ Other: _____

## Venues

- ○ Shared meetings
- ○ Campus events
- ○ Library receptions
- ○ Faculty orientations
- ○ Faculty meetings
- ○ Teaching and learning events
- ○ Appointments
- ○ Phone calls
- ○ Emails
- ○ Other: _____
- ○ Other: _____

| In what venues might you connect with this partner? | What do you need to know before connecting with this partner? |
| --- | --- |
| | |
| | |
| | |
| | |
| | |
| | |

## Elevator Speech Components

1. The library offers [*service, expertise, or resource*].

   _____

2. This service, expertise, or resource contributes to [*institutional focus area*].

   _____

3. (**Optional**) We have evidence/data that confirms this contribution. For example, [*succinct explanation of evidence/data*].

   _____

4. If you participate in this service, expertise, or resource, you will [*explanation of benefit*].

   _____

5. Therefore, you should [*action you want partner to perform*].

   _____

6. I would love to help you [*take that action*].

   _____

## Elevator Speech for Partner

_____

_____

_____

**THINK**

How did this activity make me feel?

_____

_____

What questions do I have?

_____

_____

What do I want to learn more about?

_____

_____

What innovative ideas have emerged?

_____

_____

**TALK**

What does this mean for my library? For me, as a librarian?

_____

_____

What do we need to do differently, as a library?

_____

_____

What does this make me want to continue to do, do better, or do differently, as a librarian?

_____

_____

**TARGET**

| Action | Timeframe | Responsible Parties | Follow-Up |
|---|---|---|---|
| **Options to Consider**<br>• Contact colleague<br>• Make decision<br>• Take action<br>• Ask question<br>• Get evidence/data | **When to Do It**<br>• Today<br>• This week<br>• This month<br>• This semester<br>• This year<br>• 2-3 year plan | **Who to Involve**<br>• Students<br>• Staff<br>• Librarians<br>• Administrators<br>• Faculty | **What to Do Next**<br>After I complete this action, what's the next step? |
| | | | |
| | | | |
| | | | |
| | | | |
| | | | |

ACTIVITY #47

# CONSIDERING ASSESSMENT MANAGEMENT SYSTEMS

**GETTING ORGANIZED**

## Goal
Consider the functions of an assessment management systems.

## Why
To evaluate and select assessment management systems, librarians need to consider their functions and match those functions with library requirements.

## Directions
1. Consider the functions of an assessment management system.
2. Check off desirable functions.
3. Respond to the Reflection Questions.
4. Engage the **T3** process.

## Suggested Readings

Hutchings, Pat. "The New Guys in Assessment Town." *Change* 41, no. 3 (2009): 26–33.

Keeling, Richard P., Andrew F. Wall, Ric Underhile, and Gwendolyn J. Dungy. *Assessment Reconsidered: Institutional Effectiveness for Student Success.* International Center for Student Success and Institutional Accountability, 2008.

Oakleaf, Megan. *The Value of Academic Libraries: A Comprehensive Research Review and Report.* Chicago: ACRL, 2010. 45–46, 94.

RiCharde, R. Stephen. 2009. "Data Management and Data Management Tools." In *Assessing Criminal Justice/Criminology Education: A Resource Handbook for Educators and Administrators.* Chapel Hill, NC: University of North Carolina Press.

Shupe, David. "Significantly Better: The Benefits for an Academic Institution Focused on Student Learning Outcomes." *On the Horizon* 15, no. 2 (2007): 48–57.

## Assessment Management Systems

○ Collect and serve as a repository for assessment evidence/data.

○ Organize evidence/data by outcome.

○ Facilitate connections between outcomes used in different units, departments, programs, and divisions.

○ Link evidence/data vertically (within units, departments, programs, and divisions) and horizontally (across units, departments, programs, and divisions).

○ Maintain record of progress.

○ Create action plans.

○ Generate reports suitable for internal purposes (e.g., strategic planning, program review, annual reports) and external requirements (e.g., accreditation documents).

○ Enable participation of staff, faculty, and administrators institution-wide.

○ Document progress toward institutional focus areas.

○ Segment evidence/data for detailed analysis.

○ Build curriculum maps.

○ Support "closing the loop" processes.

○ May integrate evidence/data from existing information systems.

○ May capture student-level evidence/data.

○ May connect to learning management systems.

## Reflection Questions

1. Which of these functions are most important to you?

_____

_____

_____

_____

2. What institutional partners may be interested in collaborating on the purchase, development, or use of an assessment management system?

_____

_____

_____

_____

3. Which of these functions are most important to institutional partners?

_____

_____

_____

_____

4. Without an assessment management system, how else might you accomplish these functions?

_____

_____

_____

_____

**THINK**

How did this activity make me feel?

_____

_____

What questions do I have?

_____

_____

What do I want to learn more about?

_____

_____

What innovative ideas have emerged?

_____

_____

**TALK**

What does this mean for my library? For me, as a librarian?

_____

_____

What do we need to do differently, as a library?

_____

_____

What does this make me want to continue to do, do better, or do differently, as a librarian?

_____

_____

**TARGET**

| Action | Timeframe | Responsible Parties | Follow-Up |
|---|---|---|---|
| **Options to Consider** <br>• Contact colleague <br>• Make decision <br>• Take action <br>• Ask question <br>• Get evidence/data | **When to Do It** <br>• Today <br>• This week <br>• This month <br>• This semester <br>• This year <br>• 2-3 year plan | **Who to Involve** <br>• Students <br>• Staff <br>• Librarians <br>• Administrators <br>• Faculty | **What to Do Next** <br>After I complete this action, what's the next step? |
|  |  |  |  |
|  |  |  |  |
|  |  |  |  |
|  |  |  |  |
|  |  |  |  |

## ACTIVITY #48
# REPORTING RESULTS

**TAKING ACTION**

### Goal
Report the results of assessment or research activities.

### Why
To maximize the impact of assessment or research activities, librarians need to communicate and disseminate results to stakeholders.

### Directions
1. Consider your (existing or anticipated) assessment or research results. What stakeholder groups want or need to know about your results?
2. Consider communication strategies or formats. Which are most likely to appeal to your stakeholders?
3. Anticipate your next presentation of results. Complete the preparation checklist.
4. Engage the **T3** process.

### Suggested Reading
Oakleaf, Megan. *The Value of Academic Libraries: A Comprehensive Research Review and Report.* Chicago: ACRL, 2010. 90–92.

### See Also
Activity #2: Stakeholders as the Heart of the Institution
Activity #51: Closing the Loop

1. What stakeholder groups want or need to know about your results?
   - ◯ Participants and target audiences
   - ◯ Interested parties
   - ◯ Responsible parties
   - ◯ Influencers
   - ◯ Decision-makers
   - ◯ Action-takers
   - ◯ Strategic planners
   - ◯ Other: _____
   - ◯ Other: _____

2. What are the goals, needs, outcomes, or institutional focus areas of greatest interest to these stakeholders? How are your results related to these interests?

   _____

3. What communication media strategy or content format is most likely to appeal to these stakeholders?

**Media**

- ◯ Executive summary
- ◯ Annual report
- ◯ Newsletter or newspaper
- ◯ Email
- ◯ Meeting or presentation
- ◯ Bookmark
- ◯ Poster
- ◯ Website
- ◯ Other: _____
- ◯ Other: _____

**Content**

- ◯ Text
- ◯ Graphics, visualizations
- ◯ Tables and charts
- ◯ Quotations and narratives
- ◯ Qualitative focus
- ◯ Quantitative focus
- ◯ Formative focus
- ◯ Summative focus
- ◯ Short time or length
- ◯ Long time or length
- ◯ In person
- ◯ In print
- ◯ Online
- ◯ Other: _____
- ◯ Other: _____

## Presentation Preparation Checklist

O  Stakeholder:

_____

_____

O  Key message:

_____

_____

O  Relevant goals, needs, outcomes, or institutional focus areas:

_____

_____

O  Research or assessment method/tool:

_____

_____

O  Evidence/data to support message, including limitations:

_____

_____

O  Interpretations and conclusions drawn from evidence/data:

_____

_____

O  Recommended decisions and actions for improvement, including timeframes:

_____

_____

O  Requested stakeholder participation:

_____

_____

**THINK**

How did this activity make me feel?

_____

_____

What questions do I have?

_____

_____

What do I want to learn more about?

_____

_____

What innovative ideas have emerged?

_____

_____

**TALK**

What does this mean for my library? For me, as a librarian?

_____

_____

What do we need to do differently, as a library?

_____

_____

What does this make me want to continue to do, do better, or do differently, as a librarian?

_____

_____

**TARGET**

| Action | Timeframe | Responsible Parties | Follow-Up |
|---|---|---|---|
| **Options to Consider**<br>• Contact colleague<br>• Make decision<br>• Take action<br>• Ask question<br>• Get evidence/data | **When to Do It**<br>• Today<br>• This week<br>• This month<br>• This semester<br>• This year<br>• 2-3 year plan | **Who to Involve**<br>• Students<br>• Staff<br>• Librarians<br>• Administrators<br>• Faculty | **What to Do Next**<br>After I complete this action, what's the next step? |
|  |  |  |  |
|  |  |  |  |
|  |  |  |  |
|  |  |  |  |
|  |  |  |  |

# MANAGING THE MESSAGE

**RE-THINKING**

### Goal
Analyze the degree to which library communications emphasize library contributions to institutional focus areas.

### Why
To maximize stakeholder awareness of library contributions to institutional focus areas, librarians need to intentionally and continuously manage the "message" delivered via library communications.

### Directions
1. Identify library communications delivered to stakeholders, including annual reports, website screen shots, newsletters, brochures, signage, bookmarks, etc.
2. Select and affix two examples of library communications.
3. Consider the institutional focus area to which your library contributes.
4. Using a highlighter, circle or underscore the parts of each example that communicate library impact on institutional focus areas.
5. Respond to the Reflection Questions.
6. Engage the **T3** process.

### See Also
Activity #1: Institutional Focus Areas
Activity #2: Stakeholders as the Heart of the Institution
Activity #26: Library Impact Map

Affix communication example #1 here.

## Reflection Questions

1. Which institutional focus areas does this library communication include? List.

   _____

   _____

2. How does this communication depict the library's contribution to institutional focus areas?

   _____

   _____

3. Roughly what percent of this communication emphasizes library contributions to institutional focus areas?

   _____

   _____

4. How might this communication do a better job aligning the library with institutional focus areas?

   _____

   _____

Affix communication example #2 here.

## Reflection Questions

1. Which institutional focus areas does this library communication include? List.

   _____

   _____

2. How does this communication depict the library's contribution to institutional focus areas?

   _____

   _____

3. Roughly what percent of this communication emphasizes library contributions to institutional focus areas?

   _____

   _____

4. How might this communication do a better job aligning the library with institutional focus areas?

   _____

   _____

**THINK**

How did this activity make me feel?

_____

_____

What questions do I have?

_____

_____

What do I want to learn more about?

_____

_____

What innovative ideas have emerged?

_____

_____

**TALK**

What does this mean for my library? For me, as a librarian?

_____

_____

What do we need to do differently, as a library?

_____

_____

What does this make me want to continue to do, do better, or do differently, as a librarian?

_____

_____

**TARGET**

| Action | Timeframe | Responsible Parties | Follow-Up |
|---|---|---|---|
| **Options to Consider**<br>• Contact colleague<br>• Make decision<br>• Take action<br>• Ask question<br>• Get evidence/data | **When to Do It**<br>• Today<br>• This week<br>• This month<br>• This semester<br>• This year<br>• 2-3 year plan | **Who to Involve**<br>• Students<br>• Staff<br>• Librarians<br>• Administrators<br>• Faculty | **What to Do Next**<br>After I complete this action, what's the next step? |
|  |  |  |  |
|  |  |  |  |
|  |  |  |  |
|  |  |  |  |
|  |  |  |  |

# TRANSFORMING LIBRARY FACT SHEETS

### Goal
Translate traditional input and output facts into expressions of library contributions to institutional focus areas.

### Why
To express library contributions to institutional focus areas, librarians need to emphasize library impact over decontextualized facts or data points.

### Directions
1. Identify and affix a library "fact sheet" or list of library data points.
2. Select one fact or data point; enter it in the left column labeled "How Good the Library Is."
3. Transform the fact or data point into a sentence describing "What Good the Library Does or Enables Others to Do"; enter it in the right column.
4. Repeat for additional facts or data points.
5. Engage the **T3** process.

> 66 When [leaders] try to determine the return of their investment [in the library], they do not ask, 'How good is the library?' Rather they ask, 'How much good does the library do?'
>
> —JAMES MATARAZZO AND LAURENCE PRUSAK

Affix library "fact sheet" here.

| How Good the Library Is | What Good the Library Does or Enables Others to Do |
|---|---|
| | |
| | |
| | |
| | |
| | |
| | |
| | |
| | |

**THINK**

How did this activity make me feel?

_____

_____

What questions do I have?

_____

_____

What do I want to learn more about?

_____

_____

What innovative ideas have emerged?

_____

_____

**TALK**

What does this mean for my library? For me, as a librarian?

_____

_____

What do we need to do differently, as a library?

_____

_____

What does this make me want to continue to do, do better, or do differently, as a librarian?

_____

_____

**TARGET**

| Action | | Timeframe | Responsible Parties | Follow-Up |
|---|---|---|---|---|
| **Options to Consider**<br>• Contact colleague<br>• Make decision<br>• Take action<br>• Ask question<br>• Get evidence/data | | **When to Do It**<br>• Today<br>• This week<br>• This month<br>• This semester<br>• This year<br>• 2-3 year plan | **Who to Involve**<br>• Students<br>• Staff<br>• Librarians<br>• Administrators<br>• Faculty | **What to Do Next**<br>After I complete this action, what's the next step? |
| | | | | |
| | | | | |
| | | | | |
| | | | | |
| | | | | |

# CLOSING THE LOOP

## Goal

Engage the results of assessment or research activities to "close the loop."

## Why

To maximize the impact of assessment or research activities, librarians need to anticipate and interact with the resulting data and evidence in order to "close the loop."

## Directions

1. Consider potential sources of assessment and research results; add any that are missing.

### Institutional

- ○ VSA, VFA, or U-CAN data
- ○ Local, institutional, student, faculty, alumni survey data
- ○ NSSE, FSSE, BCSSE, CCSSE data
- ○ Learning management system data
- ○ Educational/professional test data
- ○ CLA, CAAP, ETS Proficiency Profile test data
- ○ IPEDS data
- ○ Institutional reporting data
- ○ Assessment management system data
- ○ Other: _____
- ○ Other: _____

### Library

- ○ Local library survey data
- ○ Service quality data
- ○ Academic Library Services data
- ○ Accreditation data
- ○ Vendor data
- ○ Learning outcomes data
- ○ Other: _____
- ○ Other: _____

2. Consider your (existing or anticipated) assessment or research results. Are they formatted in a way you can understand?
3. Engage the questions under each area: Reflect, Act, Decide, and Share.
4. Engage the **T3** process.

## See Also

Activity #48: Reporting Results

## Reflect

What are the main points, ideas, or issues revealed by these results?

_____

_____

_____

What are the limitations of these results? How do they impact the utility of the results for decision-making and action-taking?

_____

_____

_____

What do you wish you knew that these results do not tell you?

_____

_____

_____

## Decide

What decisions can you make as a consequence of these results?

_____

_____

_____

Who can you include in the decision-making process?

_____

_____

_____

_____

Who can you include in the decision-deployment process?

_____

_____

_____

## Act

What actions can you take as a consequence of these results?

_____

_____

What can you do differently or better?

_____

_____

What can you continue doing?

_____

_____

What can you start doing?

_____

_____

What might you change the next time you conduct similar assessments?

_____

_____

## Share

Who wants to know about these results?

_____

_____

Who needs to know about these results?

_____

_____

What is the best venue, method, or format for sharing these results?

_____

_____

What decisions or actions do you want to occur as a consequence of sharing these results?

_____

_____

**THINK**

How did this activity make me feel?

_____

_____

What questions do I have?

_____

_____

What do I want to learn more about?

_____

_____

What innovative ideas have emerged?

_____

_____

**TALK**

What does this mean for my library? For me, as a librarian?

_____

_____

What do we need to do differently, as a library?

_____

_____

What does this make me want to continue to do, do better, or do differently, as a librarian?

_____

_____

**TARGET**

| Action | Timeframe | Responsible Parties | Follow-Up |
|---|---|---|---|
| **Options to Consider** <br> • Contact colleague <br> • Make decision <br> • Take action <br> • Ask question <br> • Get evidence/data | **When to Do It** <br> • Today <br> • This week <br> • This month <br> • This semester <br> • This year <br> • 2-3 year plan | **Who to Involve** <br> • Students <br> • Staff <br> • Librarians <br> • Administrators <br> • Faculty | **What to Do Next** <br> After I complete this action, what's the next step? |
| | | | |
| | | | |
| | | | |
| | | | |
| | | | |

**ACTIVITY #52**

# ARTICULATING THE INSTITUTIONAL VALUE OF THE LIBRARY

GETTING ORGANIZED

### Goal

Summarize the library's value, impact, and contributions to institutional focus areas.

### Why

To communicate with stakeholders effectively, librarians need to articulate library value, impact, and contributions to institutional focus areas clearly and concisely.

### Directions

1. Draft, in your own words, a statement summarizing library value, impact, and contributions to institutional focus areas.
2. Revise your drafts, tightening your message and maintaining stakeholder perspectives.
3. Practice your delivery.
4. Engage the **T3** process.

### Suggested Reading

Oakleaf, Megan. *The Value of Academic Libraries: A Comprehensive Research Review and Report.* Chicago: ACRL, 2010. 91.

**Draft**

**Revision**

**THINK**

How did this activity make me feel?

_____

_____

What questions do I have?

_____

_____

What do I want to learn more about?

_____

_____

What innovative ideas have emerged?

_____

_____

**TALK**

What does this mean for my library? For me, as a librarian?

_____

_____

What do we need to do differently, as a library?

_____

_____

What does this make me want to continue to do, do better, or do differently, as a librarian?

_____

_____

**TARGET**

| Action | Timeframe | Responsible Parties | Follow-Up |
|---|---|---|---|
| **Options to Consider**<br>• Contact colleague<br>• Make decision<br>• Take action<br>• Ask question<br>• Get evidence/data | **When to Do It**<br>• Today<br>• This week<br>• This month<br>• This semester<br>• This year<br>• 2-3 year plan | **Who to Involve**<br>• Students<br>• Staff<br>• Librarians<br>• Administrators<br>• Faculty | **What to Do Next**<br>After I complete this action, what's the next step? |
| | | | |
| | | | |
| | | | |
| | | | |
| | | | |